"Stephen Mattson has a finger on the pulse of current cultural climate and also demonstrates robust theological acumen. His writing consistently draws us to keep the main thing the main thing: Jesus. Love. Resistance. I'm thankful for Mattson's clear and prophetic voice."

—CINDY WANG BRANDT, author of *Parenting Forward*

"In the most recent census, 30 percent of 18- to 29-year-old respondents marked 'none' under religious affiliation. There is growing evidence that the majority of these young people are not alienated from Jesus—merely from the church. *The Great Reckoning* is useful for offering an alternative way of approaching Christian faith that will appeal to many who are unhappy with Christendom but hungry for Christ. Stephen Mattson raises important and provocative questions for believers to consider."

—ALEXIA SALVATIERRA, author of *Faith-Rooted Organizing*

"Stephen Mattson is doing important work here. He is entering the cumbersome layers of time, tradition, and dogma and excavating Jesus from beneath them. He doesn't deny the real ugliness of Christianity's recent past, but he uncovers the more beautiful truth of what it first meant to follow Jesus—and he does so with wisdom, honesty, and compassion. *The Great Reckoning* will be a wonderful companion for those on the journey of losing religion and finding faith."

—JOHN PAVLOVITZ, author of *A Bigger Table*

D0916066

"The Trump era has convinced many people of what they've long expected: the Christian faith has been hijacked. Political agendas, corrupt institutions, culture wars, and hypocrisy have poisoned a religion struggling to emulate the person of Jesus. In *The Great Reckoning*, writer Stephen Mattson navigates the difference between Christendom and Christ, and offers a way back toward the latter."

—BENJAMIN COREY, author of *Unafraid* and *Undiluted*

"All I can say after reading *The Great Reckoning* is *ouch*! But what a good, necessary, godly, beautiful, Lord-I-needed-this-badly kind of ouch it was! Thank you, Stephen Mattson, for not just calling out the mess, but offering a way out of it. You left me inspired, shaken, and convicted into action. And now it's my turn to walk the way of Christ the way Christ intended it to be walked."

—CARLOS A. RODRÍGUEZ, author of *Drop the Stones* and founder of HappySonship.com

"From this important book we glean this word: instead of leaning into a failing American Christianity that has always oppressed, we lean into Christ."

—KAITLIN CURTICE, activist and author of *Glory Happening*, from foreword

the GREAT RECKONING

the GREAT RECKONING

Surviving a Christianity That Looks Nothing like Christ

STEPHEN MATTSON

Herald
P R E S S

Harrisonburg, Virginia

Herald Press
PO Box 866, Harrisonburg, Virginia 22803
www.HeraldPress.com

Library of Congress Cataloging-in-Publication Data
Names: Mattson, Stephen, author.
Title: The great reckoning : surviving a Christianity that looks nothing like
    Christ / Stephen Mattson.
Description: Harrisonburg : Herald Press, 2018.
Identifiers: LCCN 2018020002| ISBN 9781513803401 (pbk. : alk. paper) |
    ISBN 9781513803418 (hardcover : alk. paper)
Subjects: LCSH: Christianity--21st century. | Christianity and culture. |
    Christianity--United States. | Christianity and culture--United States.
Classification: LCC BR481 .M293 2018 | DDC 277.3/083--dc23 LC record avail-
able at https://lccn.loc.gov/2018020002

THE GREAT RECKONING
© 2018 by Herald Press, Harrisonburg, Virginia 22803. 800-245-7894.
    All rights reserved.
Library of Congress Control Number: 2018020002
International Standard Book Number: 978-1-5138-0340-1(paperback);
    978-1-5138-0341-8 (hardcover); 978-1-5138-0342-5 (ebook)
Printed in United States of America
Cover and interior design by Reuben Graham

22 21 20 19 18   10 9 8 7 6 5 4 3 2 1

To
Emily Mattson,
Miriam Mattson,
Ian and Ruthie North,
and Jackie Sommers.

Thank you for everything.

Contents

Foreword

It's a confusing time to be a Christian. Many of us in the United States are asking, How did we get here? What happened along the way?

Yet it's important to note that this isn't the first or last time that we will struggle with our identity. To look at our present circumstances as the church, we've got to constantly look backward. We need to pay attention to our role as Christians throughout history. Stephen Mattson mentions in *The Great Reckoning* that the church has often seemed to support justice—while practicing injustice. In the United States right now, we have to reconcile that truth if we want to truly follow after Jesus.

As a Potawatomi woman who follows the teachings of Jesus, I struggle with this every day of my life. How do I reconcile what the church has done to ancestors of Indigenous peoples while still believing that the church can do what's right for future generations? We live with a history of stealing Native children and putting them in boarding schools. Those children were forced to convert to a version of Christianity that I do not want to have any part in. So how do I reconcile my own faith? And how do we reconcile with each other, keeping love and grace intact?

"I am simply trying to comprehend how I can keep loving Christ despite the sins of the church that bears his name," writes Mattson. As a white Christian man, Mattson is trying to enter into that tension: to generate honest conversations, to repent, to lament, and to ask how we can possibly move forward together as Christians. Moving forward means that we continue to overthrow oppression. It means that we continue to fight against injustice on the individual and communal level, because that is what Jesus did.

"So Jesus knows what it's like to be hurt in the worst possible way by those who claim to follow God," Mattson tells us. "If you have been hurt by religious institutions and religious people, Jesus has a holy empathy with you. Jesus shares in your suffering." This is a word to the oppressed, to the hurting. And it's also a reminder that Jesus sits in our suffering with us. That means that Jesus also sits with us in our individual and collective healing.

Mattson reminds us of the power of Pentecost—that people of many nations and tongues gathered together and were seen and known by God in their individual beauty. We are called back to the idea of Pentecost, even today. We are called to remember that everyone belongs to God, that everyone is seen and known in their own languages, their own cultures, their own joys and struggles. "Oppressing others is incompatible with following God," Mattson says, and this has to be at the core of who we are as the church today.

So from this important book, we glean this word: instead of leaning into a failing American Christianity that has always oppressed, we lean into Christ. We lean into the person who fought to topple oppressive systems and who stands on the side of the oppressed. We lean into Jesus' story, and we let that guide us forward.

I stand with my brother to do just that. I hope and pray you'll join us.

—Kaitlin Curtice, activist and author of *Glory Happening: Finding the Divine in Everyday Places*

1

Disillusioned

The Lord is near to the brokenhearted and saves the crushed in spirit.
—PSALM 34:18

At no time in my life was I more immersed in white evangelical Christian culture than during college. I was studying to become a youth pastor at a small but prominent Christian university called Moody Bible Institute. At Moody, everyone is required to be Christian, and students must sign a doctrinal statement agreeing to follow a set of rules and regulations based on so-called Christian morals and conduct. I spent most of my time attending church, studying theology, playing in worship bands, reading Scripture, and participating in an array of ministries and organizations.

We weren't allowed to watch television in our dorm rooms or see R-rated movies anywhere. We weren't permitted to have facial hair, or wear pants that were too wrinkled, or be off campus after eleven at night. Our evangelical Christian bubble was regulated by "biblical" laws, inspired by "biblical" expectations, and facilitated through "biblical" authority structures.

As a young man passionately trying to follow God, I loved it.

But while I was at Moody, September 11 happened. Terrorists hijacked planes, brought down the Twin Towers, and forever changed the course of American history. The United States was suddenly waging a war against terror, and my classmates and I were turning to God for answers with a newfound sense of urgency and desperation. Such violent death and destruction wasn't supposed to happen in our homeland! So we prayed for our country, prayed for our soldiers, and sang "My Country 'Tis of Thee" in our churches.

As an energetic, all-American college student, I desperately wanted to contribute to the war effort. So after finding an old mattress and dragging it into my dorm's lobby, I propped it against a wall and used a black magic marker to draw a human outline on it. Then, having gathered all the sharp knives I could find from dorm kitchens, I stood about twenty feet from the mattress and planted my feet in position. I hurled one knife, and then another, and then another at the guy on the mattress.

The terrorist.

It wasn't long before other students joined me. With a ruthless vengeance, we chucked knives, forks, makeshift spears, chairs, recycling bins, and anything else that wasn't nailed down at the terrorist. On the numerous occasions that I stabbed homemade weapons into the mutilated bedding, I visualized cutting open a jihadist's stomach, spilling his blood, and ripping out his guts.

Soon long lines of Bible students were eagerly awaiting their chance. What became known as the "anti-terrorist camp" quickly became a popular attraction for guys on campus. Throwing knives requires a certain amount of skill and a lot of practice. Being college students with nothing better to do, we became quite good at it. We threw, we sliced, and we stabbed. Eventually it turned into a game of "Who can make the knife stick into the terrorist from the farthest away?" With a morbid passion inspired by hate, patriotism, and fear, we unleashed violence upon this unnamed Islamic enemy and defended our country—God's country—from evil forces.

The anti-terrorist camp lasted for days. Every morning we'd pretend to torture and kill hundreds of Muslim terrorists. Then we'd go to our classes and learn about God. Later in the day we might even walk the streets of Chicago and evangelize to strangers, telling them about the wonderful love of Jesus.

So there I was: a bloodlusting, hate-filled, revenge-seeking Christian. But that's how nearly everyone I knew was. I remember how I felt during that time: confident, holy, righteous, and assured that everything I believed in was right.

WHEN CHRISTIANS ARE WRONG

But I was wrong. I was nowhere close to reflecting the character of Jesus.

Jesus: a Middle Eastern man. Jesus: a Savior who forgave people's sins. Jesus: the Messiah, who commanded his followers to love their neighbors as they love themselves.

Jesus: God who came to earth to lovingly sacrifice himself for enemies—not gleefully kill them.

Fully engulfed in white evangelical Christian culture, I was thinking and acting in ways that were totally anti-Christ. My

entire religious system—or at least the religious people surrounding me—affirmed this depravity and actually prodded
me further from the reality of Jesus. Our knife hurling and
terrorist hating were all done under the guise of Christianity.
We wrapped our faith and our nationalism into one great big
package: national security, justice, judgment, a holy nation,
Christian America, demonic Islam. "Something needs to be
done about the innocent people being killed by terrorists!" "I
don't want Muslims wiping out Christianity!" "This is a sign
of the end times!" "And for crying out loud, my loved ones
aren't going to be the next victims!"

So it was that we, Christians following the Prince of Peace,
advocated bombing our enemies to death and asking questions later. To God be the glory. God bless America.

Like adherents of many popular movements, we molded our
faith on the principles of wealth, political gain, comfort, and
power, which were all disguised and spiritualized. Christ's gospel of love was manipulated as a means to an end and became
a way to justify our worldly desires and fool ourselves into
believing we were being godly. Instead of love-based power,
we were advocating for a worldly power. We believed getting
power was preferable to giving power, and that taking life was
better than sacrificing our own. We entrusted our souls to the
kingdoms of the world instead of to the kingdom of God.

My Christian faith at that time—and for a few years after—
was so radically different from the life of Jesus as documented
in the Bible that one might wonder how the two could ever
possibly be reconciled. Yet I didn't even wonder about the dis-
crepancy. Millions of us didn't wonder. Instead of seeing our
world through the lens of Christ, we saw our Christ through
the lens of our own religious worldview.

While much has changed since 9/11, much has also stayed the same. To this day, lots of Christians—many of whom I love and admire—defend such thoughts and actions as reasonable and justifiable. But reading the accounts of Jesus' life in the New Testament has made it increasingly hard for me to rationalize such sentiments. I have changed. Some of my loved ones would say I've changed for the worse, but I think it's been for the better. For the very first time in my entire life, I'm starting to understand that Christianity is about Christ.

That sentence—*Christianity is about Christ*—may seem painfully obvious. But when you attend a church that doesn't welcome you, or listen to pastors who are preaching hate, or see theologians banter on social media, or watch evangelists spew lies on television, or see Christians engage negatively with the culture around you—well, you would be justified in thinking that Christ is absent from much of Christianity.

When Christianity no longer looks like Christ, the act of advocating for the least of these—refugees, immigrants, the maligned—might be met with fierce and often hateful resistance. When Christianity looks nothing like Christ, sacrificial love is replaced with brute force, and allegiance to Jesus is supplanted by allegiance to nation. Christians then support policies that block refugees from entering their country, deport people instead of embracing them, continue to funnel billions into a military-industrial complex that expands across the globe, and passively allow systemic racism and inequality. Rather than look to Christ for guidance, they embrace immoral leaders who care more about acquiring power than loving others.

Looking back, I realize that as I held a knife in my hands and prepared to hurl it at the image of a human being, Jesus was conspicuously missing from my mind and heart. I should have noticed that then. But I didn't notice, and neither did legions of other self-proclaimed Christians. Throughout history, Christians have been guilty of abandoning the virtues of the Jesus they claim to follow. Christians have even been the key instigators and players in some of the world's most evil movements. The Crusades. The exploitation and genocide of Indigenous peoples. The Holocaust. Slavery, segregation, and white supremacy.

The list could go on and on. Time and again, Christians throughout history have gotten it wrong. We continue to get it wrong today.

WHAT DO YOU MEAN BY "CHRISTIAN"?

Christianity could mean a million different things to a million different people. Whenever someone asks if you're a Christian, you might want to ask what they actually mean when they say "Christian." Author Sarah Bessey notes, "In some circles, using the word 'Christian' is the equivalent of saying you're a racist, homophobic, climate-change denying ignoramus ready to storm a women's health clinic to murder a doctor."[1] The biggest problem with defining Christianity is that everyone has wildly differing ideas of what it actually is.

Let's consider a few terms. The word *Christianity* describes the religion surrounding the teachings, life, death, and resurrection of Jesus. The word *Christian* comes from the Greek word *Christianos*, which means "follower of Christ." *Christian* has become an adjective in contemporary conversation—a way to describe not only a person who follows Jesus but also a modifier for a family, a corporation, and even an entire nation. For example, because they're closed on Sundays and espouse conservative "family values," businesses like Chick-fil-A and Hobby Lobby are deemed to be "Christian" companies. Starbucks's support for LGBTQ (lesbian, gay, bisexual, transgender, and queer) communities casts it, in the minds of many, as a non-Christian business. Strangely enough, in this way it becomes possible to identify a chicken sandwich and shabby-chic picture frame as somehow "Christian" and a disposable coffee cup as not.

Christendom, then, is a form of Christianity that has gained cultural and social and political dominance. Christendom blesses and is blessed by the political realm in which it enjoys widespread popularity. Christendom dates back to the fourth century, when Constantine made Christianity the dominant religion of an entire empire and used the faith to justify and sanction violence and warfare. Christianity has never been the same. Christendom still reigns wherever the church blesses the state and the state smiles on the church. Christendom is present whenever Christian culture becomes dominant. We'll look at this more in a later section.

Evangelical Christianity is a particular brand of Christianity that emphasizes personal conversion, the centrality of the cross, the authority of the Bible, and evangelism. _White evangelical Christianity_, which is represented by the majority white culture, has become a dominant force in U.S. politics and public life and a primary driver of Christendom as it is experienced in the United States today.[2]

"Religion is man-made," the famous atheist Christopher Hitchens once declared. "Even the men who made it cannot agree on what their prophets or redeemers or gurus actually said or did."[3] Hitchens saw little that was good in Christian faith. But Christopher's own brother, author Peter Hitchens, believes that Christianity is one of the best things to happen to humanity. "Only one reliable force stands in the way of the power of the strong over the weak," writes Peter Hitchens. "Only one reliable force forms the foundation of the concept of the rule of law. Only one reliable force restrains the hand of the man of power. And, in an age of power-worship, the Christian religion has become the principal obstacle to the desire of earthly utopians for absolute power."[4]

Here we have two brothers who are both talking about the same thing—Christianity—yet have polar views of what it represents. Which brother is correct? They both are. Christianity is as various as the people who adhere (or don't adhere) to it.

Indeed, anybody can call themselves—or anything else—"Christian." Adolf Hitler once said, "I believe today that I am acting in the sense of the Almighty Creator."[5] Hitler obviously wasn't a follower of Jesus, but at the time many thought that he was, partly because he implemented Christian rhetoric in his speeches and propaganda. While we may easily dismiss the idea that Hitler was a Christian, the very fact that he was able to use Christianity to serve his evil purposes should prompt us to reflect seriously upon our own world. What might we be mistakenly identifying as "Christian" today? The label of Christianity can fulfill sinful desires, and Christianity can be misused for many deplorable purposes. In Christendom, Christianity comes in handy for raising campaign donations, increasing business, acquiring fame, and justifying the shaming, hurting, and even killing of others.

Exploiting Christianity is as old as Christianity itself; it's a tactic that's been employed throughout history. The original deception that Satan used to fool Adam and Eve was an attempt to pass wickedness off as being godlike. Satan promised Eve, "You will not surely die. For God knows that when you eat of it your eyes will be opened, and you will be like God, knowing good and evil" (Genesis 3:4-5). Many have been similarly deceived, being presented with a religion they mistakenly perceive as representing Christ when in reality the "Christianity" they're experiencing, and possibly even living, is a lie.

Frederick Douglass clearly witnessed this type of deception when the white Christianity of his day widely participated in slavery. He offered this accurate indictment:

> Between the Christianity of this land and the Christianity of Christ, I recognize the widest possible difference—so wide that to receive the one as good, pure, and holy, is of necessity to reject the other as bad, corrupt, and wicked. To be the friend of the one is of necessity to be the enemy of the other. I love the pure, peaceable, and impartial Christianity of Christ; I therefore hate the corrupt, slave-holding, women-whipping, cradle-plundering, partial and hypocritical Christianity of this land. Indeed, I can see no reason but the most deceitful one for calling the religion of this land Christianity.[6]

White Christians spiritualized slavery with a bold confidence. In *The Great Stain: Witnessing American Slavery*, author Noel Rae notes how white Christians of that era used the Bible to rationalize the evil of owning slaves, citing Old Testament references and using verses like Ephesians 6:5-7 ("Slaves, obey your earthly masters . . ."). Rae quotes Stephen Elliott, a bishop who presided over the Episcopal Church in the Confederacy, as an example of how many put a positive spin on it:

Around Sierra Leone, and in the neighborhood of Cape Palmas, a few natives have been made Christians, and some nations have been partially civilized; but what a small number in comparison with the thousands, nay, I may say millions, who have learned the way to Heaven and who have been made to know their Savior through the means of African slavery! At this very moment there are from three to four millions of Africans, educating for earth and for Heaven in the so vilified Southern States—learning the very best lessons for a semi-barbarous people—lessons of self-control, of obedience, of perseverance, of adaptation of means to ends; learning, above all, where their weakness lies, and how they may acquire strength for the battle of life. These considerations satisfy me with their condition, and assure me that it is the best relation they can, for the present, be made to occupy.[7]

In that way, the evil of slavery was presented as a form of Christian goodness. White evangelical Christianity still lives with the legacy of its justification of slavery, and dominant Christianity continues to issue theological statements and rationalizations that downplay or disregard the injustices related to incarceration, inequity, income inequality, and immigration. Decades from now, will the American Christianity of our day be known for a legacy of inspiration, or will its stance on racism, refugees, immigration policy, welfare, gender, and poverty leave a damning mark in history? We must always be vigilant and aware of how Christianity is being co-opted.

In 1993, over seventy people died after federal agents stormed a compound in Waco, Texas, after a fifty-one-day siege. Inside the compound were Branch Davidians, a group of religious followers led by David Koresh, who claimed to be a messiah figure and used biblical references and symbolism to establish a cult following. Using the books of Ezekiel and Revelation, Koresh manipulated people into believing they were being faithful followers.[8]

In 2018, an offshoot of the Unification Church in Pennsylvania held a ceremony in which members were to bring their "rods of iron"—a reference from the book of Revelation that they interpret to mean guns—to participate in a bizarre ceremony. Members were asked to bring AR-15s and other semiautomatic rifles to the church service. Hundreds of people participated, many wearing robes and adorned with crowns, some of which were made of rings of bullets.[9]

While these cases are extreme examples of twisting the Bible almost beyond recognition, any religious community—given the right mix of fear and ignorance—is susceptible to molding faith to fit its own narratives. Most Christians would never consider joining such outlandish groups as the Branch Davidians or the AR-15-toting churchgoers, but most have probably been guilty of subtly tweaking their faith to cater to their own desires. Whether we're conscious of it or not, we've all adjusted our view of God for our own benefit.

THE GOODS OF THE FAITH

Few things are worse than experiencing the empty and destructive forms of the Christian religion. We will look at many of these forms in this book. But Christianity can also be indescribably wonderful. Some of my very best memories are of church and of knowing that I was loved by a Christian community. Ever since I was a baby crawling around in the church nursery, Christianity has given me amazing friends. Twenty-six years after my parents first carried me to church, I married Emily, who had been a baby in that same nursery. Our wedding was held in that exact same church, surrounded by hundreds of our family and friends.

There are unimaginable blessings to following Jesus, and as countless people will attest, being a Christian can be life-changing in the best possible way. The Bible promises that "the one who trusts in the Lord, whose confidence is in him . . . will be like a tree planted by the water that sends out its roots by the stream. It does not fear when heat comes; its leaves are always green. It has no worries in a year of drought and never fails to bear fruit" (Jeremiah 17:7-8 NIV). The apostle Paul affirms that "God will supply every need of yours according to his riches in glory in Christ Jesus" (Philippians 4:19). As if to leave no doubt regarding the benefit of following God, Paul also declares that "no eye has seen, nor ear heard, nor the heart of man imagined, what God has prepared for those who love him" (1 Corinthians 2:9).

Pursuing a relationship with Jesus is amazing. Jesus has dramatically transformed the lives of billions of people worldwide. Despite racial, cultural, and political differences, countless individuals throughout history have discovered the awesome reality of God. When you consider thousands of years of shared testimonies and traditions that have been experienced through Christ, it's almost beyond belief. These innumerable witnesses to God's glory across history and the globe serve as evidence of the richness of Christianity. God, through the power of the Holy Spirit, enlivens people's spiritual lives and the work of the church.

Christianity is commonly cast as either the villain or the hero of history. Both are oversimplifications. Much like the Hitchens brothers demonstrate, the reality is that Christianity can be both a bad force and a good one. We see this dichotomy within

Christianity all the time. Members of one church may picket a funeral, while members of another volunteer at a homeless shelter. One pastor may spout racist ideologies, while another works tirelessly to combat white supremacy. One Christian coworker may steal your lunch from the break room refrigerator, while another may buy you lunch on the day you forgot to bring one. The good and the bad can be contained within a single Christian too! A follower of Jesus may lie to you in the morning and offer help and encouragement later in the afternoon. Honest self-reflection shows that the difference between being Christlike and un-Christlike can be a matter of a few seconds. One moment we may be sitting peacefully in traffic, and the next moment we have become road-rage monsters.

So who decides what is "Christian" and what's not? Who decides what the gospel is and what it isn't? God does, and the Bible proclaims that everything good and holy has been embodied in the person of Jesus Christ. The apostle Paul states, "For in Christ all the fullness of the Deity lives in bodily form" (Colossians 2:9 NIV). The writer of Hebrews says, "[Jesus] is the radiance of the glory of God and the exact imprint of his nature, and he upholds the universe by the word of his power. After making purification for sins, he sat down at the right hand of the Majesty on high" (Hebrews 1:3).

The life of Jesus may be interpreted differently by various people, but it will never change. It's there for us to see, prophesied about in the Old Testament and forever captured by the gospels of Matthew, Mark, Luke, and John. Jesus serves as a witness to the eternal and unchanging character of God. The Bible points toward—and is centered on—Jesus. Jesus is what God looks like. Jesus is who we're supposed to emulate, and Jesus is the point of the entire Christian story.

Amid all the confusion surrounding Christianity, I've learned that putting Jesus as the focal point of your faith is a life-giving source of inspiration and hope. As obvious as this may seem, many people abandon their Christian faith because they mistake the murky labels of Christianity as being the same thing as Christ. But like all religions, Christianity is an imperfect substitute for God. Pastor Bruxy Cavey reflects this point when he suggests, "I do not believe all religions lead to God because no religion leads to God. Religion does not lead people to God any more than cups quench your thirst."[10] Jesus came to replace religion with himself, Cavey says. When we promote any form of Christianity instead of God, we introduce people to a set of religious beliefs and moral guidelines. They can find Christian friends, get involved with a Christian church, work at a Christian organization, read Christian books, listen to Christian music, attend Christian conferences, but still never actually know Christ.

NAMING CHRISTIAN CULTURE

What is Christian culture? Simply put, *culture* itself is the set of beliefs and customs and ways of thinking that characterize a particular social, organizational, national, ethnic, or age group. Christian culture, then, consists of the behaviors, beliefs, institutions, things, and people associated with Christianity. When that culture gains a measure of social power in the wider society, that's Christendom. It's important for Christians and non-Christians alike to understand the drastic difference between dominant Christian culture and Christ. Jesus and the cultures and subcultures that claim to represent him are not the same thing.

A person can be totally immersed in Christian culture without ever actually discovering Christ. When many leaders and institutions within Christian culture claim to reflect Christ, represent Christ, and even embody Christ, it can be difficult to figure out the truth. So if you're going to a church or believing in a brand of faith that doesn't correlate with the example of Jesus, it might be time to reassess.

Not everyone who claims to follow Jesus actually does. We can see why people are turned off by the Christian faith, because it frequently doesn't look anything like Jesus. Being immersed in Christian environments means witnessing Christian individuals, churches, and organizations failing to live up to Christ's example. In the 1980s, televangelists Jim and Tammy Faye Bakker were caught using their Christian entertainment empire to scam hundreds of thousands of dollars from people. Sordid accounts of Jim's extramarital affairs and the Bakkers' extravagant lifestyle eventually led to their downfall. Having duped millions of people into believing they exemplified what it means to live a holy life, the Bakkers were the public faces of American Christianity. For many, their downfall served as a lesson: Be skeptical of public displays of religion. Never take Christians at face value. Today, when celebrity pastors like Joel Osteen, Benny Hinn, and Creflo Dollar use ministries to buy private jets, Rolls-Royces, and mansions and write books with titles like *You're Supposed to Be Wealthy: How to Make Money, Live Comfortably, and Build an Inheritance for Future Generations*, Christians lose credibility.[11]

Spirituality is a grueling series of spiritual wins, devastating losses, and frustrating draws. Christians will fail in their faith, and so will you. For many, it's hard to recover a sense of trust in a faith after so many violations. Many never will. So how can followers of Jesus save themselves from self-destruction?

For many, the solution to any Christian-related problem has always been to pray harder, read the Bible more, worship longer, and increase your church involvement. Pray. Read the Bible. Worship. Attend church. Repeat. Eventually, the theory goes, these practices will inevitably help strengthen your faith by deepening your relationship with God. As healthy as these spiritual disciplines are, however—and they are undeniably good—they don't always work magically to remove despair and cynicism. Without truly discovering God, we will find all religious good intentions to be meaningless.

Investing our faith in the shadow of the real thing—worshiping Christendom instead of Christ—is easy to do, because Christian culture has become an industry that focuses on itself rather than God. Fix your marriage by signing up for a couples' retreat—$200. Become a better parent by attending next month's How to Raise a Teenager Conference—$400. Experience true worship by buying tickets to Praise Fest (sponsored by your local Christian radio station)—$75.

Christendom's solution for any spiritual struggle is to dive deeper into itself. Before long it becomes our god, and we can no longer differentiate between Christendom and the God it has replaced. And when we mistake Christendom as being the same thing as Christ, we glorify Christian culture, follow Christian culture, sacrifice for Christian culture, worship Christian culture, and convert people to Christian culture—even as we ignore the Christ at the center.

Both Christians and non-Christians have been victimized by Christian culture, and many have been unable to put a name to their victimization. Both current and former followers of

Christ can find it hard to identify exactly why their faith sputtered, burned out, or went through phases where it seemed frustratingly devoid of anything good. At its very best, Christendom is a flawed representation of Christ; at its very worse, it can be a destructive force. If we aren't careful, we can make Christian culture an idol, a quasi deity and spiritual entity we praise and love. We can make it our king and protect it as if it's our own kingdom.

RECKONING WITH REALITY

Endless resources exist for the sole purpose of helping Christians grow spiritually. Yet hardly any practical advice exists for actually surviving Christianity itself. Most Christian media and educational content—with few exceptions—are built around the premise that Christendom is good and the secular world is bad. But the idea that dominant Christian culture itself is imperfect and sinful? That is difficult for many believers to imagine.

For many of us, however, the struggle is no longer how to survive a secular culture. It is how to survive Christianity itself.

The Great Reckoning is intended to help followers of Jesus in this current cultural moment, in which so many Christians are reckoning with the sad realities of what "Christianity" has become. Similar to the Great Awakening, a series of revivals that permanently affected the Christian faith for years to come, I believe that we are living in what we could call the Great Reckoning: a time of soul-searching and truth-seeking and candid reflection on what we as Christians have allowed Christianity to become. We do not yet know where the Great Reckoning will lead us. And it may take a long time to get there.

"Two thousand years ago God started a revolt against the religion He started," writes author Erwin McManus. "So don't ever put it past God to cause a groundswell movement against churches and Christian institutions that bear His name. . . . I am convinced that there is an uprising in the works and that no one less than God is behind it."[12]

In today's partisan climate, people might wonder if this book caters to Democrats or Republicans, or if it's attempting to attract theological progressives or traditionalists. Frankly, *The Great Reckoning* is meant to confront these assumptions altogether, navigating through these constant influences that insert agendas into Christianity. The goal is to decipher what Christ meant his followers to be about by studying who we have become.

I'm not naïve. I know some people will think some parts are "too liberal" and others will find some parts "too conservative." My hope, however, is that this book will guide us back to centering our faith on Christ. We'll look at the differences between Christ and Christendom, and we'll assess and critique the Christian religion with honesty and transparency, intimately dissecting it to levels of discomfort. We'll expose Christian subcultures that foster abuse and oppression and will challenge their ideological biases. We'll praise and chastise Christianity, describing it in a manner that captures all its complexity. Most importantly, *The Great Reckoning* is about finding hope and restoration through Jesus, and discovering how that can be done in a practical way. "Throughout the history of Christianity, Jesus has been a source for good, for shalom, for peacemaking, for justice keeping," writes author Kaitlin Curtice. "But the institution of the church has made mistakes. We criticize the church because we want to see it made more whole, because we want to heal the world of its wounds and to admit that it starts with us."[13]

Like countless Christians, I am trying to decipher what is of Christ and what is not. I am learning to reckon with the reality of what my faith has become. Like many other followers of Christ today, I am simply trying to comprehend how I can keep loving Christ despite the sins of the church that bears his name.

2

Sins of the Church

If we say we have no sin, we deceive ourselves, and the truth is not in us. If we confess our sins, he is faithful and just to forgive us our sins and to cleanse us from all unrighteousness. If we say we have not sinned, we make him a liar, and his word is not in us.

—1 JOHN 1:8-10

When was the last time you heard a confession in church? When have you heard a Christian or a group of Christians apologize for something? Anything?

Corporate and individual confession have been long-standing Christian practices, but publicly admitting to and asking forgiveness for sin has become a lost discipline. "If we confess our sins, he is faithful and just to forgive us our sins and to cleanse us from all unrighteousness," writes John in 1 John 1:9, reaffirming the wonderful joy and confidence we can have from knowing that God has defeated sin through Jesus' death and resurrection. James also encourages us to "confess your sins to one another and pray for one another, that you may be healed. The prayer of a righteous person has great power as it is working" (James 5:16).

Corporate confession of sin has become so rare in some segments of the church that it's nearly extinct. Some faith communities do regularly and effectively make an effort to confess and repent, but the number is dwindling. Most Protestant churches don't have confessionals. Regardless of denomination, few modern church services offer a purposeful time for confession. Musical worship? Check. Offering? Check. Sermon? Scripture? Announcements? Check. Check. Check.

Public or private confession of sins? (Crickets chirping.)

One study found that only 2 percent of Catholics still practice confession on a monthly basis—this from a tradition that has confession as one of only seven sacraments.[1] On the rare occasion when a confession does occur anywhere within Christendom, it's usually only after a wrongdoing has been found out—part of the process of reconciliation, punishment, or forgiveness. We've become so used to *not* confessing that it's often shocking and disruptive when it happens.

A historic abuse of the practice of confession by the church—such as requiring indulgences and fostering an environment of shame and guilt—has played a legitimate role in its unpopularity. Confession is still abused, in more informal ways. It is not uncommon, for example, for Christians to confess or share something intimate with other believers—often in confidence—only to be unfairly ostracized for doing so. Besides both warranted and unwarranted consequences, the added burden of gossip and exclusion makes being vulnerable and open about sin a sensitive endeavor fraught with uncertainty.

Confession is also easy to fake. We know our sins, but let's be honest: it's much easier to just keep them hidden than to face the potential public backlash and repercussions of admitting to them. When it comes time for prayer requests, we might offer up something like "I'm really struggling with pride" or "I'm bitter toward my coworker this week" instead of divulging a deeper issue such as "I cheated on my taxes" or "I'm addicted to pornography." If your church has a public prayer request list, it's probably filled with appeals related to physical ailments, healing, the conversion of an unbelieving friend, and requests for strength, guidance, and wisdom. These are all good things to pray for, but prayer request lists are as notable for what they are missing as for what they contain. A false pretense of righteousness permeates many faith communities, in which moral standards seem so impossibly high because nobody ever admits to breaking them.

It is only through openness and transparency that one can be fully known. Confession is worth the risk, despite the inevitable bumps one may experience along the way. As Proverbs tells us, "No one who conceals transgressions will prosper, but one who confesses and forsakes them will obtain mercy" (Proverbs 28:13 NRSV).

Christendom prefers condemning over confessing and has a long history of passionately denouncing others while ignoring its own faults. And corporate, culturally dominant Christianity has a lot of sins to confess. Refusing to admit our corporate sins, and remaining silent in the face of injustice, is a form of active complicity. You can often tell which sins the church is most guilty of by how little attention it gives to them.

The consequences of the extinction of confession have been dire. Interestingly, roughly 74 percent of Americans today identify as Christian (and another 5 percent identify with a non-Christian religion), but almost 90 percent of Americans believe in God.[2] While a portion of those who believe in God but don't identify with a religion may have had an entirely a-religious life experience, it seems likely that a portion of them would have engaged with Christianity at some point. You can't blame those who have been disenfranchised for feeling hurt and wounded. Christians must seriously acknowledge how many people have been hurt and rejected by the church.

As the body of Christ, it's time we confess some of our gravest sins. In this chapter we look at some of the corporate sins of Christian culture through the lens of groups of people who deserve an apology and even reparations of some kind. There needs to be an honest, soul-searching reckoning with the sins of the past and the present.

For many people in these groups, any apology from the Christian church will be too little and too late. For them, the damage has already been done. For others, the specific people and institutions that need to apologize won't, and justice may never be found. Many will find mere words hollow and flippant in the face of lives already ruined.

Yet my hope is that dominant Christianity can start to realize its sins, take ownership of its wrongdoings, and work to address them. Evil will still exist behind the buttressed walls of churches, within the piles of theological textbooks, and behind the closed doors of pastors' offices. But confessing the sins of Christianity out loud—publicly testifying to the carnage that the church has sometimes left in its wake—is a critical first step to healing the wounds. And while apologizing doesn't magically fix things, any utterance that brings forms of darkness into the light is better than silence.

THE CHURCH HAS SINNED AGAINST WOMEN

Christianity has a history of manipulating the Bible to reinforce patriarchy, in which men are seen as spiritual leaders and women are to submit to their authority. This has resulted in the smothering of women's gifts of pastoral leadership and ministry. Women are intentionally excluded from roles of authority, and their truth, wisdom, and experiences have been unfairly dismissed. Toxic masculinity has invaded workplaces, schools, government, and our public spaces. Patriarchal ideologies built upon objectification, abuse, and control—ideologies often supported by churches—have caused untold harm.

Christendom is still predominantly built on male-dominated authority structures. Only 9 percent of Protestant American pastors are women. The overall ratio of women spiritual leaders is probably far less when you consider that the Roman Catholic Church has yet to officially ordain women.[3] None of this takes into consideration the countless "pastors' wives" who work (often in addition to their paid professions) in ministry roles yet receive little to no compensation.

Women make up about 50 percent of all medical school graduates, 60 percent of all accountants, and 67 percent of all psychologists. Yet despite the fact that women are doctors, surgeons, lawyers, astronauts, presidents of universities, and the heads of state, a significant number of Christian churches and denominations still forbid them from becoming pastors and ordained ministers and ban them from various positions of leadership.[4]

Furthermore, Christendom has remained regrettably silent in the face of the epidemic of harassment, abuse, and violence against women. One in three women has been a victim of domestic violence. One in six women will, sometime during her life, be the victim of rape or attempted rape. More than half of all women have been sexually harassed at their workplace, and a staggering 87 percent of women between the ages of eighteen and twenty-five say they've experienced some form of harassment.[5]

Christian leaders, on the whole, have failed to address the abuse and assault experienced by more than half of all Christian believers. When was the last time your congregation dedicated a sermon or service to sexual harassment, assault, and abuse? If you are fortunate enough to have experienced such a service, you're the exception to the rule. Despite attending all sorts of churches within a variety of denominations and despite sitting through countless sermons, I have not once heard violence against women addressed in any significant capacity. I've heard homilies on the Leviathan, the Nephilim, and the dimensions of Noah's ark. I have not heard a single sermon confronting a problem that affects nearly every woman in every congregation, and around the world.

The functions of a human resources department and the ability to rely on a third party for unbiased accountability is largely absent from faith communities. Furthermore, I've worked in ministry positions for churches, Bible camps, vacation Bible school programs, mission trips, parachurch organizations, and other Christian institutions. Only a few have required me to engage in sexual harassment training. Most have failed to communicate any sexual harassment guidelines, sexual abuse policies, preventive education, or protocols on how to notify authorities of sexual assault. Alarmingly few of the Christian institutions I have worked for have conducted background checks. Yet all of these measures were mandatory for every job I've ever held in the secular world.

Instead of taking a proactive approach against sexual assault, harassment, and abuse, Christianity has been complicit in its spread. Rachael Denhollander, the first woman to accuse USA Gymnastics team doctor Larry Nassar of sexual abuse, had this to say about churches:

> Church is one of the least safe places to acknowledge abuse because the way it is counseled is, more often than not, damaging to the victim. There is an abhorrent lack of knowledge for the damage and devastation that sexual assault brings. It is with deep regret that I say the church is one of the worst places to go for help. That's a hard thing to say, because I am a very conservative evangelical, but that is the truth. There are very, very few who have ever found true help in the church.[6]

Rather than address this widespread crisis, Christendom has created toxic and unregulated environments in which predatory men (and women) often face no consequences for their actions. Rather than publicly denouncing the perpetrators, large contingents of Christians actually support them, especially if they share similar political and spiritual beliefs. Denhollander says she found little support when she spoke out against her abuser. "Advocacy for sexual assault victims, something I cherished, cost me my church and our closest friends three weeks before I filed my police report," she said. "I was left alone and isolated. And far worse, it was impacted because when I came out, my sexual assault was wielded like a weapon against me."[7]

The false spiritual premises of patriarchy provide cover for such actions by abusers and the churches that support them. A deep-rooted misogyny, in which women are emotionally, spiritually, and physically oppressed, lies at the center of much of evangelicalism today. Denhollander's testimony underscores how presidential candidate Donald Trump could still receive 81 percent of the white evangelical vote after voters learned that he had said, "I moved on her like a [*****]. But I couldn't get there. And she was married. Then all of a sudden I see her, she's now got the big phony [****] and everything. . . . I just start kissing them. It's like a magnet. Just kiss. I don't even wait. And when you're a star, they let you do it. You can do anything. . . . Grab 'em by the [*****]. You can do anything."[8]

Instead of believing survivors, Christians blame them. Instead of rebuking the perpetrator, Christians shame those who were assaulted. If sexual abuse or assault happens within a church or involves a parishioner, many faith communities won't notify law enforcement but rather try to deal with the issue in-house, often under the pretense of "spiritual healing" or "accountability" or "reconciliation." This leaves victims without justice and culprits without punishment. Saying "I'm sorry" without any reparations is hollow.

A prominent pastor named Andy Savage was recently accused of a sexual assault that occurred roughly twenty years earlier, when he was a youth leader. The victim was a girl in the youth group at the time, and as an adult she had the courage to confront Savage by writing him a private email message. Savage never responded, so she went public. Remarkably, while still refusing to directly respond to the woman, Savage communicated only through the platform of his church. After admitting the so-called "incident" during a church service, the congregation gave Savage a standing ovation. Sadly, this type of scenario, in which the victim is ignored and the perpetrator defended, happens routinely within Christendom.[9]

The church must be held to account. The church must do better. It is incumbent upon the church to attend to the words and actions of Jesus, who treated women as equals, with the respect and love deserved by divine image-bearers of God.

In the immortal words of Dorothy Sayers:

> Perhaps it is no wonder that the women were first at the Cradle and last at the Cross. They had never known a man like this Man—there never has been such another. A prophet and teacher who never nagged at them, never flattered or coaxed or patronized; who never made arch jokes about them, never treated them either as 'The women, God help us!' or 'The ladies, God bless them!'; who rebuked without querulousness and praised without condescension; who took their questions and arguments seriously; who never mapped out their sphere for them, never urged them to be feminine or jeered at them for being female; who had no axe to grind and no uneasy male dignity to defend; who took them as he found them and was completely unself-conscious.[10]

THE CHURCH HAS SINNED AGAINST PEOPLE OF COLOR

The white church must repent of its continued sins of white supremacy. When Christianity arrived to the Americas in the form of Spanish "explorers," few Indigenous people groups survived the rampant diseases the intruders brought with them, which killed off entire populations. Those who did survive were forced to choose between converting to Christianity or enduring slavery—often with little difference between the two—and were the victims of a prolonged and genocidal campaign of oppression.[11] When Protestants eventually arrived to what would eventually become the Thirteen Colonies, they viewed Indigenous people as a threat to be either eliminated or relocated. Christian missionaries were perceived as foreign occupiers who brutally created European-style communities that attempted to erase the culture of Indigenous peoples while simultaneously converting them. As generations passed, missionary efforts to eliminate Indigenous culture through assimilation developed alongside the growing population of European invaders. Throughout it all, the Christian newcomers often violently wiped out Indigenous people, even instituting a bounty payment for scalps as an incentive to kill them off or take them as captives.[12] Eventually, through the creation of residential boarding schools and increased cooperation with the government, white Christians used their faith to supposedly "evangelize" and "civilize" Indigenous children by ripping them away from their families. They also helped to broker government land grabs and facilitate corrupt treaties that plundered the land of Indigenous populations.[13]

While all this was happening, slavery was rampant, with white Christians of means owning and trading human property. From the 1500s to the late 1800s, in addition to the estimated millions of enslaved Indigenous individuals, nearly eleven million Africans were transported to the Americas and enslaved.[14] They were captured, tortured, sold, transported, and put to work in the most horrific ways imaginable.

In all, Christendom's first appearance on this "new" continent was genocidal by nature. We must acknowledge Christianity's propensity for institutionalized racism and the subjugation of others. Being aware of this historical context is vital for Christians, especially white Christians, to understand. Professor Randy Woodley, a legal descendant of the United Keetoowah Band of Cherokee, invites Christians to "develop a

more honest history and a shalom-oriented theology, in practical partnership with the indigenous peoples of the world."
He suggests:

> The way forward is both structural and relational, re-
> quiring honest historical and theological rethinking and a
> coming to grips with the following concerns: colonialism
> and neocolonialism; the way current forms of capitalism
> resist shalom; the way racism affects our thinking and re-
> lationships; the practical implications for living on stolen
> land; how violence is thought to be needed in order to
> maintain the present system; what true reconciliation looks
> like. We need to find ways to share power, and we should
> seek to understand what justice issues are still unresolved
> among indigenous and other disempowered peoples.[15]

Reckoning with the sins of white supremacy and racial
injustice is crucial in order to prevent future sins from recurring. For example, today's xenophobia toward immigrants is
reminiscent of the era of the Chinese Exclusion Act of 1882,
during which white Americans resented Chinese workers and
blamed them for low wages and a poor economy. They used
their racist rage to push for a change in government policies,
halting Chinese immigration to the United States and prohib-
iting Chinese resident aliens from obtaining U.S. citizenship.[16]
Another well-known example is when the United States forced
persons of Japanese ancestry, including its own citizens, into
internment camps during World War II.[17] Fear is frequently an
instigator of racism but is no excuse for it.

All these injustices were done "legally," through the necessary channels of law and order, by systems favoring those in
positions of power and privilege. Throughout our nation's history, people of color have faced an inordinate amount of injustice, and still do today. Thousands of lynchings over numerous

decades demonstrate how untrustworthy the law has been for African Americans and other people of color. The discriminatory allotment of government benefits like the G.I. Bill has not only had detrimental long-term economic consequences for people of color but also reveals how federal policies can be co-opted to serve white supremacy.[18] Segregation, "separate but equal" policies, laws forbidding interracial marriage, and countless other racist practices have led to today's unjust criminal justice system, the achievement gap, wage gaps, gerrymandering, voter suppression, unfair immigration policies, deportation, international travel bans, police brutality, gentrification, and the public resurgence of white supremacists. All these are manifestations of age-old xenophobia and racism.

Throughout this entire time—stretching for hundreds of years—U.S. citizens primarily identified as Christian. Most still do. If a religion built upon Christ, who instructed his followers to radically and holistically love others, can be so thoroughly co-opted, it should come as no surprise that a government and its institutions are just as fallible.

Christendom was—and is—so embedded in American culture that you cannot dissociate it from both the past and present forms of institutional racism. Yet majority-culture Christians—white Christians—can choose whether or not to acknowledge any of this. In her critically acclaimed book *The New Jim Crow*, Michelle Alexander writes:

> When we think of racism we think of Governor Wallace of Alabama blocking the schoolhouse door; we think of water hoses, lynchings, racial epithets, and "whites only" signs. These images make it easy to forget that many wonderful, goodhearted white people who were generous to others, respectful of their neighbors, and even kind to their

black maids, gardeners, or shoe shiners—and wished them well—nevertheless went to the polls and voted for racial segregation. . . . Our understanding of racism is therefore shaped by the most extreme expressions of individual bigotry, not by the way in which it functions naturally, almost invisibly (and sometimes with genuinely benign intent), when it is embedded in the structure of a social system. The unfortunate reality we must face is that racism manifests itself not only in individual attitudes and stereotypes, but also in the basic structure of society.[19]

No matter what action white Christians take or choose not to take, it may have little to no bearing on their own reality. Privilege insulates white Christians from the immense impact that racism has on others. Conversely, no matter how people of color think, feel, or act, their reality is determined by a factor well beyond their control—their race or ethnicity. This radical contrast based simply on the color of one's skin is just one example of white privilege.[20] In some cases, the term *white privilege* itself is inappropriate—not because it's too controversial but because it's too tame and too sanitary and too individualistic. A more appropriate term may be *white supremacy*, which conveys the systemically racist nature of social structures.[21]

Every segment of American culture—the education system, the military, the government, religion, business, sports, the judiciary, law enforcement, housing, entertainment, healthcare—has been historically racist and is still racist. People of color are confronted with this sobering truth every day. But privilege allows those of us who represent the dominant power structures to ignore this reality or imagine it otherwise.

Michael Kimmel and Abby Ferber, in their book, *Privilege: A Reader*, describe it this way:

To be white, or straight, or male, or middle class is to be simultaneously ubiquitous and invisible. You're everywhere you look, you're the standard against which everyone else is measured. You're like water, like air. People will tell you they went to see a "woman doctor" or they will say they went to see "the doctor." People will tell you they have a "gay colleague" or they'll tell you about a colleague. A white person will be happy to tell you about a "Black friend," but when that same person simply mentions a "friend," everyone will assume the person is white. Any college course that doesn't have the word "woman" or "gay" or "minority" in its title is a course about men, heterosexuals, and white people. But we call those courses "literature," "history" or "political science." This invisibility is political.[22]

With few exceptions, predominantly white Christian churches and organizations have actively conspired against, ignored, or denied people of color while simultaneously ignoring, denying, or actively supporting racist and unjust behaviors, policies, and structures. As recently as this very decade, a large contingent of white Christians voted for a racist president and continue to support his racist policies, and they incorporate various maneuvers to avoid the topic of racism altogether. For white people who benefit from the societal privileges of wealth, political control, economic power, and security, acting in solidarity with people of color is optional.

But this is not an option for those who claim to follow Christ. Jesus always defended the oppressed, and his proclamation of the kingdom of God defied the corrupt ruling empires of his day. We must never negate the voice of specific groups who face injustice by downplaying their messages or deflecting attention. For example, saying "All Lives Matter" or "Blue Lives Matter" in response to "Black Lives Matter" is completely missing the point. The Bible says, "The Lord is a stronghold for the oppressed, a stronghold in times of trouble" (Psalm 9:9), and Jesus' words and actions emulated this. He made public affirmations to the world that women's lives mattered. Samaritan lives mattered. Gentile lives mattered. Blind people's lives mattered. Lepers' lives mattered. Widows' lives mattered. Orphans' lives mattered, and strangers' lives mattered—people who were regularly victimized by society. Declaring that Black Lives Matter is simply declaring a timeless truth exemplified by Jesus himself: that we should do good; seek justice, correct oppression (Isaiah 1:17).

White Christians who dismiss this fail to grasp the irony that Jesus *was* a person of color. This may come as a shock to people who assume Jesus was white, or who regularly see the Caucasian version of Jesus in books, paintings, and depictions: white, bearded, and often with blond hair and blue eyes. But forensic and historical evidence suggest that Jesus was dark-skinned and looked Middle Eastern.[23] This may be an uncomfortable truth for many Christians who benefit from never having to think about race.

We worship a Savior who was an ethnic minority unfairly arrested by law enforcement, incarcerated, and killed by police brutality. Seeing and naming that might be difficult for many Christians. But it should inspire all of us to rethink our assumptions about God and those who are made in God's image.

THE CHURCH HAS SINNED AGAINST LGBTQ PEOPLE

Imagine if a religion focused on a single attribute of humanity, decided it was evil, and demeaned an entire group of people because of it. Picture this religion consistently suggesting that individuals with this attribute are unnatural, immoral, and inherently unworthy. Envision this religion propagating falsehoods and perpetuating slanderous stories about these people: how they are dangerous to children and sexually deviant.

Few people have been more consistently harmed by modern Christianity than those who are lesbian, gay, bisexual, transgender, or queer. By devaluing their humanity and refusing to affirm their divine worth, the Christian church has repeatedly wounded those who identify as LGBTQ. The authors of *Forgive Us* put it this way: "Under the banner of protecting marriage, the church has gone on the assault against what is often called the 'gay agenda.' . . . The church must repent for attitudes and behaviors that have both wounded and demonized the LGBTQ community. After all, at the end of the day, homosexuality is not only or primarily a topic or agenda, but it is about people—millions of people who are precious in God's eyes."[24]

The American church's sin against LGBTQ people has revealed itself in countless rejections. Author Amber Cantorna confides that when she came out, her family "turned their back on me. I lost not only my parents and my only sibling, but all my extended family and a lot of my friends, my church, my hometown."[25] The church, with tactics ranging from lobbying and legislating to control the right to marry to excommunication and even physical violence, has used Christianity as a weapon against LGBTQ people.[26] Armed with a handful of what some consider to be irrefutably clear verses (note: they aren't clear at all), Christians have embarked on a holy war that is itself utterly unholy. Matthew Vines, in *God and the Gay Christian*, writes that six short passages in the Bible "have stood in the way of countless gay people who long for acceptance from their Christian parents, friends, and churches."[27] Much of the damage is unseen, with the bombardment causing a heavy psychological toll that can create long-lasting and permanent damage to the self.[28] Instead of being inclusive sanctuaries providing safety and affirmation, church communities have become shame-inducing prisons in which abuse is escalated rather than prevented.

"Many find the Church's posture and activities nothing but deplorable bigotry, little different than historic racism or sexism," writes Christian ethicist David Gushee. "The Church's image and evangelistic mission in U.S. culture have been damaged. The damage extends to many of the Church's own young people, who cringe every time the Church is identified as anti-gay, which seems to have become our defining characteristic."[29]

A large portion of Christendom remains obsessive in their persecution of those who identify as LGBTQ. It's an infatuation with judgment pursued to the most absurd levels of hypocrisy, in which LGBTQ individuals are barred from ministries, prohibited from various denominations, and actively excluded from congregations. These Christians have decided that of all the "sins" that exist in the world, being LGBTQ is deserving of the strictest of consequences. Christians who have no LGBTQ family or friends typically will have uncompromising judgments toward those who are LGBTQ but turn a blind eye to their Christian family and friends who are greedy, gluttonous, or prideful—which the Bible clearly defines as sinful. If—despite the scarcity and ambiguity of the topic within the Bible—you believe that being LGBTQ is sinful, this question must honestly be addressed: Why, above all other sins, is this the one you choose to address?

Activist Justin Lee warns: "Today's young people have gay friends whom they love. If they view the church as an unsafe place for them, a place more focused on politics than on people, we just might be raising the most anti-Christian generation America has ever seen, a generation that believes they have to choose between loving and being Christian."[30] Sadly, many Christians have been taught that there is only one truly Christian opinion about this issue and have learned to use the Bible as an excuse to dismiss the gifts and personhood of people who are LGBTQ.

It remains to be seen how Christian attitudes will unfold, but there are signs that Christianity is becoming slightly more inclusive. The Pew Research Center estimates that 51 percent of millennial evangelicals say that "homosexuality should be accepted by society" (compared to just 32 percent of their older counterparts).[31] There's a generational gap between how Christians view LGBTQ inclusiveness. The younger you are, the more likely you are to support LGBTQ rights. I believe a large part of this is because younger individuals personally know others who identify as LGBTQ, and can see for themselves the fruits of the Spirit in their friends. Younger Christians who aren't gay know that their LGBTQ friends are encouraging teammates, caring friends, trustworthy siblings, and loving parents.

All the pain and suffering caused by religious exclusion should remind Christians that practicing the love of Jesus is always more fruitful than enforcing pharisaical judgment. Theologian Sarah Coakley asks, "What orientation could be more important than the orientation to *God*, to divine desire?"

She challenges us to be "concerned with a deeper, and more primary, question: that of putting desire for God above all other desires, and with judging human desires only in that light."[32]

THE CHURCH HAS SINNED AGAINST THE POOR

Thousands of verses in Scripture clearly reference justice for the poor.[33] Proverbs 19:17 says, for example, "Whoever is generous to the poor lends to the Lord, and he will repay him for his deed." Although Christians and other religiously affiliated people do in fact give more generously to charitable causes, we still only give away about 2 to 4 percent of our total wealth.[34] That's a far cry from Jesus' instruction to "sell your possessions, and give to the needy. Provide yourselves with moneybags that do not grow old, with a treasure in the heavens that does not fail, where no thief approaches and no moth destroys" (Luke 12:33).

If we take this verse literally, it means that American Christians are among the wealthiest on earth and the poorest in heaven. But as selfish as we are with regard to the poor, few within Christendom seem to care. And why would we? We love our smartphones, luxury cars, and daily double espresso caramel lattes. To make a real sacrifice with our money—to risk our finances for something as unstable as Christ? It's not a good investment strategy.

So no matter how clear the Bible is or how loudly it proclaims God's concern for the poor, Christians in the United States appear ready to ignore its claims on our lives and wallets. And given our pastors' and leaders' unwillingness to call us to account, we know that there will be no calls for public repentance, no claims of heresy, and no public debates for ignoring the words of Jesus. Instead, Christianity reserves the op-eds, Twitter attacks, denominational splits, and Nashville Statements for issues like homosexuality and the Second Amendment.

THE CHURCH HAS SINNED AGAINST CHILDREN

Jesus treated children with the highest regard, saying that those who want to enter the kingdom must become like little children (see Matthew 18:3). The Bible says that "religion that is pure and undefiled before God the Father is this: to visit orphans and widows in their affliction" (James 1:27). When the church fails children, the damage is especially profound. We must reckon seriously with these harms.

Roughly 1 in 5 girls and 1 in 20 boys are sexually abused as children.[35] The ongoing disclosures about sexual abuse in the Roman Catholic Church shows just how prevalent this problem is within Christian communities, affecting thousands of individuals from all over the world.[36] In case after case, churches and the Christians who attended them were found to be the purveyors of crime instead of the preventers of it. Reports and allegations were never addressed or went years without formally being investigated, and an intentional effort to conceal and evade wrongdoing meant victims have rarely—if ever—received the justice they deserve.[37] To assume these problems are limited to Catholicism is naïve, and data suggests that Protestants are just as guilty of committing and covering up abuse on a similar scale. Any evil committed against children by the church is inexcusable, yet Christians continue to shy away from the accountability and work necessary to keep people safe from sexual abuse.

History will also soon judge Christianity by its inability to deal with the refugee crisis, which affects millions of children across the globe. There are currently fifty million refugee children—innocent souls desperate for food, shelter, and safety.[38] Yet in the face of this life-and-death struggle, 51 percent of Protestants (and 76 percent of white evangelicals) in the United States supported the 2017 refugee ban.[39] In doing so, they discarded verses such as "When a stranger sojourns with you in your land, you shall not do him wrong. You shall treat the stranger who sojourns with you as the native among you, and you shall love him as yourself, for you were strangers in the land of Egypt: I am the Lord your God" (Leviticus 19:33-34) and "Whoever oppresses a poor man insults his Maker, but he who is generous to the needy honors him" (Proverbs 14:31). This widespread Christian resistance to accepting refugees shows how our willingness to follow Christ is often contingent on partisan allegiance and populist fear.

Christians do a much better job of caring for children close at hand; studies show that practicing Christians are actually 50 percent more likely to foster children and twice as likely to adopt than the general public is.[40] This willingness to foster and adopt is an encouraging sign, considering there are well over four hundred thousand children in the U.S. foster care system, and goes to show that while Christians have many faults, they also have many admirable Christlike qualities.[41] Their advocacy for unborn children—despite the complexities and controversies surrounding abortion—also reveals an authentic concern for the well-being of others.

Regardless of whether those in need are refugees from afar or children near home who are waiting to be placed with a loving family, Christians have a historic opportunity to provide them with a lifetime of love and support.

THE CHURCH HAS SINNED AGAINST THE "OUTSIDER"

Christians in the United States have been known to try to force our own ethnocentric version of faith onto those from other nations. But no one group owns Christianity, and the life of Christ isn't meant to serve the nationalistic purposes of any country at the expense of others' well-being. Christ's life contradicts the values of any country, no matter its claims to be a "Christian nation," that spends billions on weapons.

Western Christians often mistake democracy for salvation and support their countries when they declare war. Rather than being peacemakers, they can become warmongers, confident in military might rather than the self-giving power of the loving God they claim to follow. Christians who are quick to denigrate immigrants, refugees, and people who are undocumented neglect verses like Exodus 23:9—"You shall not oppress a sojourner. You know the heart of a sojourner, for you were sojourners in the land of Egypt"— and Hebrews 13:2, which states, "Do not neglect to show hospitality to strangers, for thereby some have entertained angels unawares."

For many Christians living in the United States, the dark-skinned Middle Eastern man named Jesus has been replaced by a white North American male. After hundreds of years of being whitewashed, this savior's gospel isn't for the world. It's for the United States, and it has been translated through consumerism and imperialism. Rather than seeing those outside their borders as people made in the image of God, Christians in the United States often demonize them or turn them into caricatures: terrorists, economic leeches, violent radicals. Outsiders have been stereotyped as less than human. There is no room for such ethnocentrism in the kingdom of God.

THE CHURCH HAS SINNED AGAINST NON-CHRISTIANS

Non-Christians have been the victims of unfair judgment and harmed by an abusive religiosity. Whether someone is Muslim, Jewish, an atheist, or doesn't identify with any religion or non-religion, the church likely owes them an apology for how they've been treated. Made to feel unworthy and shamed, many have been ostracized through the damaging rhetoric and actions of Christendom.

Television personalities who garner millions of viewers and claim to represent Christ fuel the war against "outsiders." Preacher Pat Robertson once exclaimed, "There will never be world peace until God's house and God's people are given their rightful place of leadership at the top of the world. How can there be peace when drunkards, drug dealers, communists, atheists, New Age worshipers of Satan, secular humanists, oppressive dictators, greedy money changers, revolutionary assassins, adulterers and homosexuals are on top?"[42]

Perhaps you have faced accusations of sin and depravity when you have consumed beer or worn "immodest" clothing or because you believe in evolution. Maybe you've been warned about experiencing the wrath of God because of your beliefs or lifestyle, or maybe you have been shunned by Christians. Christians have been guilty of "relationship building" as a manipulative form of evangelism instead of just loving people for who they are—with no strings attached.

Instead of seeing non-Christians as individuals divinely created and loved by God, Christendom has made it a habit of seeing them as depraved, lost, dangerous. But maybe before we can "save" non-Christians, we must save ourselves from Christendom. We need to learn to love others—everyone—as Christ loves us.

THE CHURCH HAS SINNED AGAINST THOSE WITH DISABILITIES AND MENTAL ILLNESS

One in five people has a disability. One in five people has a mental illness. (There's some crossover between the two, because mental illness can constitute a disability). About 31 percent of all adults will experience an anxiety disorder at some point in their lives.[43] These are staggering numbers, especially given that many Christian churches are still wary of psychology as a field, perceiving it as secular. Many churches lack the basic tools and resources to help people struggling with mental health issues and those with disabilities. Just as churches have often failed to give attention to sexual harassment and abuse, churches have not taken much initiative to gain any further education or awareness regarding disabilities and mental health.

The consequences are unfortunate. Within churches— places meant to be welcoming and accessible and support- ive—only 43 percent of parents of children with disabilities felt that their faith communities were supportive. More than half had to keep their children from attending a church activ- ity because of a lack of congregational support.[44] Christians have historically explained disabilities as being the result of sin. Some Christians used to believe that the sin of the parents was a possible cause for a child's disability.

Thankfully, that attitude has lost popularity, yet many still make the theological claim that a disability is an indirect result of sin or the "fall of Adam." These rationalizations add a hurtful stigma and undeserved sense of guilt and shame, and they help to explain why many people with disabilities feel shunned by various churches. Both physical and mental health issues have been dangerously spiritualized, and medical diag- noses have been characterized as faith-related.[45] Desiring God, a prominent Christian ministry founded by John Piper, recently tweeted, "We will find mental health when we stop staring at the mirror and fix our eyes on the strength and beauty of God."[46] There was immediate backlash to the insinuation that mental health is somehow related to someone's spiritual state, as if people can just "pray away" depression or have enough faith to make everything better. When Christians disregard scientific and medical research, they put the lives and health of others in danger by using spiritual rhetoric to convince people to avoid proper healthcare.

I've talked to people who have been persuaded that they were "called by God" to stop taking their meds or who have quit therapy because someone in their church suggested it. The results, including serious relapses and regressions, have been disastrous. Years of progress were erased by spiritual whims. In many cases, unqualified leaders attempt to replace the work of licensed counselors and health professionals, to the detriment of those who need professional help.

Although the Americans with Disabilities Act requires most institutions to make accommodations for those with disabilities, many are exempt. Instead of intentionally working to be as inclusive as possible, faith leaders have preferred to put their time, money, and resources elsewhere, further alienating a community that should be an essential part of the church. Sadly, in a study of church attendees, 25 percent said they were unsure (or even disagreed with the idea) that people with disabilities were even created in the image of God.[47]

Some may claim it doesn't make sense for churches to build wheelchair-accessible entryways or have a person with a disability read Scripture or organize a support group for those who struggle with debilitating anxiety. Theologically, these things make all the sense in the world. We must be like the people described in Luke 5, who did whatever it took for their friend to access the love of Christ—even if it meant cutting a hole in a roof.

LAMENTING CHRISTIANITY'S MISTAKES

When Christendom caters to the powerful masses rather than the forgotten minorities, the message of Jesus loses its power. Jesus did the exact opposite of many modern churches. He was unafraid to go against cultural norms, and those who follow him into the kingdom of God are inefficiently obsessed with including everyone. This is why Jesus, the Good Shepherd, will leave the ninety-nine sheep in order to search for the one who is missing.

Those of us living within Christendom tend to gloss over misdeeds that need to be admitted and wrongs that should be corrected. The book of Ecclesiastes reminds us that there is a season for everything, even a time to weep and mourn (Ecclesiastes 3:1-8). For Christians, mourning is an important spiritual practice. Author Soong-Chan Rah writes, "For American evangelicals riding the fumes of a previous generation's assumptions, a triumphalist theology of celebration and privilege rooted in a praise-only narrative is perpetuated by the absence of lament and the underlying narrative of suffering that informs lament." Rah continues, "The American church avoids lament. The power of lament is minimized and the underlying narrative of suffering that requires lament is lost. But absence doesn't make the heart grow fonder. Absence makes the heart forget. The absence of lament in the liturgy of the American church results in the loss of memory. We forget the necessity of lamenting over suffering and pain. We forget the reality of suffering and pain."[48] Allocating time and energy to naming Christianity's mistakes is necessary for those wishing to spread the gospel of Christ. Jesus overturned the temple tables in fury, disgusted by how something meant to be holy had become rotten. Sometimes the wrongdoings of Christendom must be reckoned with. Sometimes the tables must be overturned.

At some point in our lives, whether directly or indirectly, most of us have been hurt by Christians and the religion they represent. This is true whether you are a Christian or not. In 2010, bestselling author Anne Rice posted this on her Facebook page: "For those who care, and I understand if you don't: Today I quit being a Christian. I'm out. I remain committed to Christ as always but not to being 'Christian' or to being part of Christianity. It's simply impossible for me to 'belong' to this quarrelsome, hostile, disputatious, and deservedly infamous group. For ten years, I've tried. I've failed. I'm an outsider. My conscience will allow nothing else."[49] Rice's sentiment is shared by many believers. There are many who deserve apologies who aren't listed here, but that doesn't mean they aren't owed one. If this includes you, your pain is real, and your anger and frustration against Christendom is legitimate. You may never get the recompense you deserve from Christianity. You may never receive the apology you deserve.

Yet even if Christianity rejected you or a loved one, Christ hasn't. And he never will. Christ himself was betrayed by religion too. For it was the religious institutions of Jesus' day that killed him. The Pharisees—the highest of priests and most honored spiritual leaders who ruled the places of worship— were considered righteous and holy. They were the ones who transferred Christ from the bondage of the religious empire to the bondage of a political one, where he was legally put on trial and sentenced to death.

Publicly humiliated, flogged, beaten, spat on, Jesus was betrayed by his closest friends. One friend betrayed him for just a few pieces of silver, and another by denying, on three separate occasions, that he knew him. Eventually his disciples abandoned him while he was sent to be tortured on a cross, where he was mocked, ridiculed, and deliberately drained of life in a way that only Roman soldiers could do. Jesus died a form of death gruesomely perfected to be the most painful experience possible.

So Jesus knows what it's like to be hurt in the worst possible way by those who claim to follow God. If you have been hurt by religious institutions and religious people, Jesus has a holy empathy with you. Jesus shares in your suffering.

3

When Christianity Hurts

My God, my God, why have you forsaken me? Why are you so
far from saving me, from the words of my groaning? O my God,
I cry by day, but you do not answer, and by night, but I find
no rest.

—PSALM 22:1-2

As a shy four-year-old boy, I felt comfortable only at home and at my family's church. My uncle was the pastor, and the charismatic congregation—consisting of a few hundred people—was filled with relatives and friends I'd known since birth. My parents were devout members, and we attended services every Sunday morning, Sunday evening, and Wednesday night—along with a litany of small groups, Bible studies, picnics, and potlucks.

While my three older siblings actually enjoyed socializing at church—hanging out with their friends any chance they could—I preferred to attach myself to my mom. Although I knew everyone at church, I was too anxious to leave her side. Despite my crippling social fears, however, I liked church. I knew God was there. Plus, I was convinced that Jesus was truly the only person keeping my family and me alive. Jesus protected us from car crashes, diseases, animal attacks, and bad dreams while simultaneously helping me get good grades and eat my vegetables. I prayed fairly constantly, following the instructions of my Sunday school teachers, who told us that God could hear us pray no matter where we were—even underwater! I feared that if I stopped praying my entire family would suddenly die, so I rarely stopped.

The only thing I did more than pray, in fact, was pick my nose. Ever since I was a baby, I had the unbreakable habit of sticking my fingers into my nostrils. (My own kids seem to have inherited this unfortunate trait.) Despite my mother's constant nagging, and her lightning-quick hands that pulled my fingers away, it was a vice I simply couldn't overcome.

One Sunday morning, I arrived at church and followed the usual routine: I tightly gripped my mother's hand, greeted a few relatives, and accompanied my parents to our customary seats. Since kids weren't dismissed for the King's Kids children's pro-gramming until midway through the service, I had to endure about forty minutes of the service before getting released to go eat snacks, view flannelgraph presentations about shepherds, and watch videos about Salty the Singing Songbook.

As I sat waiting for the service to begin, I plopped down in my seat, sprawled out, and began to pass the time by picking my nose, just like any other kid would do. As fate would have it, a stranger approached my family and started walking down our aisle. With my index finger up my nostril, I became aware that the man was heading to greet my parents. So I quickly

took my finger out of my nose, wiped the seaweed-colored res-
idue beneath my seat, and opened a hymnal. The man greeted
my parents and then moved along to meet other families who
were gathered and also waiting for the service to begin. Then
he walked to the very front row of the sanctuary and sat next
to my uncle, who gave him an enthusiastic pat on the back.

Sitting in the front row of our church next to my uncle
was a sacred honor. It meant that you were either a pastor, a
special speaker, or a missionary. Turns out that this guy was all
three. His sermon would be followed by a goodwill offering to
financially support his ministry. And because it was a special
message, children would not be dismissed for King's Kids but
would instead get to listen to a real-life missionary.

I slouched down in the pew and prepared to endure an eter-
nity of boredom. When it was the missionary's turn to speak,
he told stories of dangerous wars, rough terrain, and people in
faraway lands. It was all very fascinating . . . until he started
talking about the children who went to church in the place
that he now lived.

They loved to read their Bibles (just like me), pray to God
(just like me), and attend church (just like me). I thought these
things were wonderful, and I imagined that I'd like the children living in this far-off place. But then the tone of his voice
lowered and he furrowed his brow and began speaking sternly
about the respect the children had for their church and elders.
They were respectful and obedient. All the time.

He then started preaching about things like television
shows, dancing, drugs, and alcohol. The congregation nodded
their heads in somber recognition. He lectured about schools,
discipline, sex, swearing, profane music, and secular movies.
He gave more and more examples of our morally failing society.

Suddenly he paused and stared right at me. "And this morning, when I came into church," he said, drama edging his voice, "I met a boy who was lying across his seat and picking his nose!" He pointed toward where I was sitting. Everybody in the congregation nodded, agreeing with the missionary. There were titters of laughter. Yes indeed, today's modern kids— more specifically, the boy he pointed at—were proof of our country's wicked decay.

Have you ever experienced a moment when time seems to stop? That's how it felt that morning. I didn't move. I was too mortified to cry. I felt embarrassed, humiliated, and deeply ashamed. For the first time in my entire life, I didn't feel safe in church.

In fact, at that very moment, church was the scariest place on earth.

I now see that my humiliation that day is a metaphor, of sorts, for the way that people are shamed and hurt by the church all the time. Church no longer felt safe or welcoming to me. I was a child, and the moment passed quickly. But for many people who have been wounded by the church, the agony takes place over years and decades.

In the last chapter we looked at some of the specific groups against which the church has sinned and who have been wounded by the church. We'll now look at a few brands of Christianity that bring hurt into the lives of its adherents. We'll also examine a few ways of viewing the gospel that attempt to avoid the pain of life but end up *increasing* it for many Christians.

THE PROSPERITY GOSPEL

While few publicly admit to following the prosperity gospel, many believe in its grand promises and enticing hope.

Christianity is perceived as a divine benefits package—a God-sponsored insurance plan—that guarantees a "blessed" future. In its most obvious forms, the prosperity gospel promises increased wealth and riches. But a far more subtle—and prevalent—version of the prosperity gospel is a distaste for discomfort.

Many churches, even those that don't broadcast the "health and wealth" message of the prosperity gospel, promote Christianity as a quick and painless solution to all of life's problems. Instead of introducing Christianity as a path to having a relationship with God, it becomes a product that promises much while requiring little. It's easy to succumb to a faith that's full of fun, entertainment, and never-ending happiness. Anything disrupting this bliss is swept under the rug or simply ignored.

Brokenness can thrive within such circumstances. Many believers are also afraid to admit that their faith is imperfect, and put up a facade of happiness that pretends nothing bad ever happens within Christianity. Some fear that if people find out our Christian lives are actually broken, non-Christians will be scared away. So we hide our flaws, mistakenly believing that we're glorifying God and somehow "protecting" God from bad press. But instead of saving Christianity's reputation, we're dishonoring God and setting ourselves up for failure.

This form of gilded Christianity hides from—or completely ignores—the harshness of a broken world, despite the fact that the life of Jesus clearly dictates engagement with brokenness. Adherents to the prosperity gospel struggle to rationalize doubt and suffering as anything other than a divine form of punishment. Natural disasters like hurricanes are interpreted as God punishing people for some sort of sin. Believers of this type of gospel view their own power as a blessing from God, believing the lie that one of God's main purposes is to satisfy humanity's worldly desires. Christianity simply becomes a means to an end, a sort of cosmic good luck charm that enables people to afford a new car, watch their favorite sports team win the championship, receive the promotion at work they've always wanted, and become popular. In this arena, pastors are self-help gurus, sermons are motivational speeches, and the religion of Christianity is a cash cow—a golden calf.

In his book *Disappointment with God*, author Philip Yancey quotes a friend who said, "We tend to think, 'Life should be fair because God is fair.' But God is not life. And if I confuse God with the physical reality of life—by expecting constant good health for example—then I set myself up for crashing disappointment."[1] Contrary to a life of ease, Christianity demands sacrifice and a lifetime dedicated to loving others. This can be difficult, and it is a commitment not meant to be taken lightly. Christianity isn't a form of escapism, and Christ's gospel isn't about ignoring conflict but about confronting it.

PRIVILEGED CHRISTIANITY

Western churches prove that political control, legislative influence, and military dominance don't equate to spiritual authority. Much like the biblical narratives of the Israelites demanding an earthly king, communities that seek carnal power often lack spiritual power. Privileged church communities—those with the most money and influence—can afford to sit back and do nothing, because they aren't the ones being victimized by the policies they support.

How many times have we heard Hallmark-esque platitudes in the midst of real tragedy? How many times have we heard nothing at all, receiving silence when looking to the church for guidance? When white supremacists marched in Charlottesville, Virginia, carrying torches and inflicting violence, many churchgoers discovered a sobering reality: their faith communities didn't care about racism. When sexual assault became an international conversation, many churches and their leaders remained silent. Whether in regard to another mass shooting or an immoral president, people of faith are often quiet and passive for the sake of maintaining their own personal convenience.

In the face of human suffering, God is not glorified by denial, or false hope, or the pretense that things are not as bad as they seem. In a world filled with wars, diseases, hatred, and injustice, Christianity should never hide under the idol of religion.

Tony Campolo exhorts the church by exclaiming, "Jesus never says to the poor, 'Come find the church,' but he says to those of us in the church: 'Go into the world and find the poor, hungry, homeless, imprisoned.'"[2] It's often the poor, hungry, homeless, and imprisoned from whom the most prophetic voices arise, and by whom the truths of Christ are most cherished and proudly proclaimed.

Spiritual awakening is rarely created by the dominant political groups or ruling social classes. Instead, it originates from the marginalized, from those crying out to God for hope and justice and deliverance. God is attentively listening to the oppressed, and Christians should do the same. If groups of people say they're being victimized, the church should believe them rather than criticize them. Christians should offer help instead of judgment.

Perhaps there's no better example of this than the cold reception that Black Lives Matter has received from many white Christians. Despite the evidence of income inequality, racial profiling, staggeringly disproportionate incarceration rates, well-documented cases of police brutality, and a palpable history of suffering under systemic racism, many white Christians refuse to recognize that there's a problem. When Black Lives Matter (a movement that around 80 percent of African Americans support[3]) decides to protest or speak out against such travesties, white Christians should join in solidarity. But instead, the truth about injustice is co-opted by other narratives.

Activist Shaun King describes well this dichotomy of a cruel Christendom versus a loving Christ: "Personally, I am finding it increasingly difficult to be a *Christian*. Not because I've stopped believing . . . but because I find it very difficult to claim to be a part of the same religion of millions, tens of millions, of people who openly state that they hate me, hate the cause I am a part of, and hate hundreds of millions of people I love and care about."[4]

Christians must identify and admit to their privilege in order to follow Christ. By doing so, an inclusive and empowering faith will take root, and the nativist tendencies of old can finally be overcome. In his book *Prophetic Lament: A Call for Justice in Troubled Times*, Soong-Chan Rah writes, "In the American Christian narrative, the stories of the dominant culture are placed front and center while stories from the margins are often ignored." Rah points out that "any theological reflection that emerges from the suffering 'have-nots' can be minimized in the onslaught of the triumphalism of the 'haves.' What do we lose as a result of this imbalance? American Christians who flourish under the existing system seek to maintain the existing dynamics of inequality and remain in the theology of celebration over and against the theology of suffering."[5]

This role reversal, in which the powerful are upstaged by the humble, is best exemplified by Jesus himself, who time and again went out of his way to prove that "the last will be first, and the first last" (Matthew 20:16). Pope Francis insists that he prefers "a church which is bruised, hurting and dirty because it has been out on the streets, rather than a church which is unhealthy from being confined and from clinging to its own security."[6]

This is how the gospel of Christ works: by empowering the lepers, the lame, and the blind while admonishing Rome and all its rulers.

FEARMONGERING

A gospel that prefers comfort over the realities of the world has an equally destructive counterpart: fear. Some versions of Christianity view faith as a brutally hard prison in which freedom is only earned through the impossible task of appeasing a perpetually disappointed God. With only a few "true Christians" existing within a fallen and hopeless world, humanity will never meet God's standards. This worldview assumes that God is more angry than loving and that disease, war, and other negative events may be well-deserved judgments of a person's or a country's sins.

In his book *Unafraid: Moving beyond Fear-Based Faith*, author Benjamin Corey writes, "For all the unintended consequences of some expressions of the Christian religion, I think fear is the most devastating—because fear has a way of permeating all areas of our lives . . . and a faith rooted in the fear of God will bring death to places inside us that we didn't even know could die."[7]

Fearmongers prey on our most basic insecurities and vulnerabilities. Fear of being rejected, anxiety about the future:

these can be manipulated into a type of anxious spirituality. Taking advantage of cultural and political conflict, a fear-monger vilifies others and passes along judgments to anybody willing to listen. Fear smothers hope to death and torpedoes our decision-making ability. In much the same way the ten fearful spies ruined God's plan for the Israelites to inherit the Promised Land, we squander our chances to bravely trust in God's goodness.

Imagine if Christians throughout North America whole-heartedly embraced refugees, intensely lobbying for their admittance into our countries, our neighborhoods, and our lives. But fear is often louder than the still, small voice of God. Warnings about how refugees might be terrorists, criminals, and a drain on our economy trigger worries and corrupt hope. Fear always imagines what will go wrong instead of what will go right.

Doom-and-gloom spirituality has resulted in books, movies, and an entire market that sells—at quite a profit—to people addicted to fear. From people holding up signs that read "Gays Will Burn in Hell! REPENT NOW!" at stadium entrances to the preacher angrily shouting a sermon during the bus commute, fear-driven theology is everywhere. Pastor John Hagee recently turned apocalyptic prophecies, lunar eclipses, and biblical "signs" about the end times into a bestselling book called *The Four Blood Moons*. It's not the first time Christian authors have cashed in on end-times rhetoric, of course. The Left Behind series and others of its ilk have longed played to the fears of Christians.

This is the unfortunate power of fear. But with God, we can overcome it. In the Bible, Joshua exhorts us to "be strong and courageous. Do not be frightened, and do not be dismayed, for the Lord your God is with you wherever you go" (Joshua 1:9).

In many ways, spiritual fearmongers are salespeople, selling a solution to the fear they're spreading. Sometimes they're literally selling something: a book about Middle Eastern prophecies, a downloadable template on how to survive a Russian invasion, holy water that protects your house from demonic powers. But this "solution" is usually a narrow belief, uncompromising in nature and exclusive in scope. Fearmongers believe they are the sole proprietors of deliverance, and those who don't strictly abide by their redemption are fated to suffer some type of wrath from God. Although they spread fear everywhere, they claim salvation can only be found by a select few. Within these strict and uncompromising environments, faith is simply a form of religious indoctrination.

A fearmongering faith is draining, sapping us of hope and inspiration. To combat this, regularly assess whether your spirituality is fueled by an optimism in God or an overwhelming despair. Evangelist and author Beth Moore offers this encouragement in the face of fear: "Over and over Jesus implores His followers, 'Take courage!' as if His hand is outstretched and His palm opened with offered treasure. It's time we took Him up on it. Do we really want to spend our time rehearsing deaths of all kinds rather than engaging in the effervescence of life?"[8]

FUNDAMENTALISM

Fundamentalism is another way that some Christians try to avoid hurt. Christian fundamentalism comes in many forms, and as with adherents of the prosperity gospel, few people openly claim—or even realize—that they're fundamentalists. Fundamentalists desperately want to be right and often assert that almost everyone else is wrong. A person's beliefs and doctrines can become immovable monuments cemented by numerous factors. Ignorance, the fear of the unknown, or even the distrust of outsiders can cause someone to prefer a faith guided by rules rather than a relationship. This can manifest itself in both "progressive" and "conservative" forms of Christianity.

Surprisingly, many fundamentalists once started out being open-minded facilitators of change. For example, some of the most ultraconservative "fundamental" churches were once deemed heretical, proving how easy it is for any sacred revolution to devolve into a stagnant religion. I've heard countless stories about my family's older generation and their "edgy" and pioneering faith. They fled Ireland, got expelled from schools, started churches, and participated in revivals. There are many colorful anecdotes, each highlighting very genuine and sacrificial acts of faith. Yet whenever my relatives reflect on today's Christian climate, they tend to bemoan modern spirituality and become critical in much the way others once criticized their forebears. In doing so, they're carrying on the long-standing prejudice of believing that the religious experiences of one's own generation are better than both those that preceded and those that follow. It's only a matter of time before my own children grow up and become old enough to gawk in disbelief at the terrible ways my generation defined Christianity. Eventually, I may also find myself assuming that *their* new ways of doing Christianity are inherently inferior to *mine*.

Anyone's spirituality can quickly deteriorate into fundamentalism, because it offers to fulfill some of our greatest spiritual desires: a defined formula for salvation, clear-cut rules, theological clarity, and a specific path to God. Fundamentalism is fueled not just by confidence in one's own faith but also by distrust and disdain for the faith of others. Fundamentalism takes comfort in certainty and finds solace within zealotry.

But fundamentalism can miss the single most important requirement of following Jesus: love. The apostle Paul testifies, "If I speak in the tongues of men and of angels, but have not love, I am a noisy gong or a clanging cymbal. And if I have prophetic powers, and understand all mysteries and all knowledge, and if I have all faith, so as to remove mountains, but have not love, I am nothing. If I give away all I have, and if I deliver up my body to be burned, but have not love, I gain nothing" (1 Corinthians 13:1-3).

The prosperity gospel, privileged Christianity, fearmongering, and fundamentalism—all attempt to deflect hurt and pain in their own way. Yet all have resulted in millions of disillusioned people who are hurting in the wake of their dominance.

TAKE HURT SERIOUSLY

Here's the thing about people being let down by Christianity: the hurt is real and the pain is deep. Christendom and Christians and religious practices—all of it—can be a painful mess. In *The Dark Side of Christian History*, Helen Ellerbe writes, "The Christian church has left a legacy, a world view, that permeates every aspect of Western society, both secular and religious. It is a legacy that fosters sexism, racism, the intolerance of difference, and the desecration of the natural environment. . . . As a result, Christianity has helped to create a society in which people are alienated not only from each other but also from the divine."[9]

Wanting to give up on Christianity isn't always a sign of immaturity, and feeling far from God doesn't mean you've done something wrong. This entire spiritual puzzle—trying to interpret what is God and what isn't, what is real and what is religious posturing, what is of Christ and what is of Christendom—requires energy and attention. Perhaps seeing this struggle as a puzzle rather than a sin will help us not discredit another person's feelings toward God. We cannot invalidate another person's experience with the church or disparage another's outlook toward Christianity.

Perhaps you have never been shamed by the church or upset at God. If that's the case, and if you find yourself confused about people's criticisms toward Christianity or upset at their combative questions, practice empathy. "Empathy is not simply a matter of trying to imagine what others are going through," writes Cornel West, "but having the will to muster enough courage to do something about it. In a way, empathy is predicated upon hope."[10]

Use your imagination to put yourself in another's shoes, and refuse to cast the first stone. There's an unwritten expectation within Christian culture that it's never acceptable to be discontented with God and that we should always be satisfied in any spiritual situation. This message is communicated through simplistic platitudes and clichés about God. If our best friend dies: "God has a reason for everything." If we lose our job: "Trust in God." If we're feeling depressed: "Rejoice in God." If we're abused: "We can't understand God's plan, and God has a reason for everything." Theologian Stanley Hauerwas writes, "Much of the Christianity that surrounds us assumes our task is to save appearances by protecting God from Job-like anguish. But if God is the God of Jesus Christ, then God does not need our protection. What God demands is not protection, but truth."[11]

Answering people's doubts or concerns or anger is not our task. God can handle our dialogue, no matter how bitter it might be, and the Bible shows us that God wants us to be truthful rather than deceitful. God prefers sincerity over pretense, and as Christians, we shouldn't trivialize anyone's hurts. The Psalms are a list of brutally honest revelations, with exclamations like "You have rejected us and disgraced us" (Psalm 44:9) and "Awake! Why are you sleeping, O Lord? Rouse yourself! Do not reject us forever! Why do you hide your face? Why do you forget our affliction and oppression?" (Psalm 44:23-24). Lamentations is a heartbreaking account of honest sorrow, in which wailing like "The Lord has become like an enemy" (Lamentations 2:5) reveals the depths of despair. "My eyes are spent with weeping," says the writer of Lamentations. "My stomach churns; my bile is poured out to the ground because of the destruction of the daughter of my people, because infants and babies faint in the streets of the city" (Lamentations 2:11).

At its essence, Scripture is a divine dictation that humans are to be authentic. If there's one thing God values over and over again, it's genuine truth. And here's some truth: Christianity can be hard. My wife and I went through a miscarriage. A few years ago one of our family's closest friends died of cancer, and many loved ones are currently battling cancer. One of my college friends committed suicide, and countless friends and family are battling depression and anxiety. I've observed people who are homeless sleeping in heaps of trash. My car has been stolen, my possessions have been vandalized, and I've been publicly humiliated and bullied, financially broke, and have often felt alone and abandoned.

My list could go on, and so could yours. Everyone has a list, and most lists are probably worse than mine, filled with unspeakable pain and suffering. I'm a privileged white male living in America, so my list is missing difficulties encountered by people who live in poverty and people of color and women around the world. No matter our background, we're going to have devastating days, weeks, months, or even years. So how does God factor into our very worst experiences? When abuse, sickness, violence, and death overwhelm us, we inevitably ask, Where is God?

TAKE QUESTIONS SERIOUSLY

When you begin to feel skeptical about faith or the church, what would it mean to interpret it as a sign of spiritual maturity rather than weakness? Not even the world's best theologians can fully explain every aspect of the Christian faith. Even after a lifetime of studying and learning, we cannot have God completely figured out. It's only natural that questions about God will continually develop throughout our lives. And what would it mean for you to shy away from being curious or to prohibit yourself from inquiring about God, the Bible, or Christian practices and traditions? Curiosity and inquiry represent a healthy intellect that builds on logic and satisfies a deep-rooted passion for finding truth.

Rather than signs that you should quit Christianity, feelings of frustration and dissatisfaction might actually be hopeful signs that you're headed in the right direction. Throughout the New Testament, we see the disciples and followers of Jesus continually getting things wrong. These are the choice words that Jesus spoke to Peter after his attempts to dissuade Jesus from pursuing his mission: "Get behind me, Satan! You are a hindrance to me. For you are not setting your mind on the things of God, but on the things of man" (Matthew 16:23).

Jesus also reproached his disciples after they wanted to call down fire from heaven in order to kill others (Luke 9:54-55), and later he "rebuked them for their unbelief and hardness of heart, because they had not believed those who saw him after he had risen" (Mark 16:14). Earlier in Mark we hear Jesus ask the disciples: "Why are you so afraid? Have you still no faith?" (Mark 4:40).

When we read the Bible as modern Christians, we take the disciples' bumbling experiences and translate them into well-packaged lessons that have been learned and passed down from generation to generation. But when we really look at the disciples' firsthand involvement with Jesus, we see that they're human. They ask questions, have doubts, become afraid, and make mistakes, just like us. Judas eventually betrayed Jesus, and Peter attacked someone with a sword. Peter also denied Jesus three times, the disciples were argumentative and prideful and indignant, and all seemed to abandon him during his greatest time of need.

When we prevent people from being real with God or invalidate their feelings about God, we're preventing them from experiencing God. We're not trusting that God is wise enough to have an answer, strong enough to face the criticism, divine enough to resolve the issue, and loving enough to restore the relationship.

Many people in the Bible—in fact, most of them—had some sort of conflict with God yet are credited as being holy and good. Abraham tries to bring about God's promise through Hagar instead of Sarah, Isaac lies about his wife, Jacob lies about his birthright, Moses doesn't want to speak on behalf of God and thereby dishonors God, Aaron makes a golden calf as a false idol, David kills his lover's husband, and Peter denies Christ (see Genesis 16, 26, 27, Exodus 4, 32, Numbers 20, 2 Samuel 11, and Luke 22). Yet in the end, despite their massive mistakes, God finds favor with those who are honest and truthful.

It has taken me years to be honest about how hurtful it was to be shamed in front of the entire congregation. It has taken me years to disentangle the words of that visiting minister, who was supposed to be God's spokesperson, from the reality of God's love for me. Thanks to models of true Christian faith, I'm learning to be candid about my disillusionment with the church and my questions about God. Knowing that God desires transparency frees us to live a faith that is both real and unassuming, providing fulfillment even amid uncertainty. The once unattainable standards associated with an idyllic Christianity are unburdened by a gracious Christ, who always prefers honest relationships over legalistic perfection.

4

Great Expectations

But the fruit of the Spirit is love, joy, peace, patience, kindness, goodness, faithfulness, gentleness, self-control; against such things there is no law.
　—GALATIANS 5:22-23

Walking into a new church for the first time can feel like attending a wedding reception and being dragged out onto an empty dance floor by a drunk groomsman. You just never know what's going to go down.

Having grown up among Christians and having visited lots of churches, I should know this by now. So a few years ago when my wife and I visited a relative's church—a charismatic congregation tucked away among the expansive fields of the Midwest—I should have known to expect something extraordinary.

The small sanctuary was packed with farmers who had lived in this small town most of their lives. That morning, one of the sixty-year-old elders of the church got up to preach. He got right to the point. "Our nation is in the midst of a dangerous era," he said. "Satan is all around us, controlling our government and moving through the countries near Asia. The end times are upon us!"

I was now on the edge of my seat, and the elder went on to explain that he had dedicated the previous decade of his life to studying prophecy, interpreting the book of Daniel and Revelation, and talking to God about the rise of the anti-Christ. He had some alarming news to share with the congregation. Needless to say, he didn't hold back. Not only was President Obama part of Satan's grand scheme to destroy America—"a godly nation"—but almost every European and Asian nation was preparing to carry out and fulfill the end-times prophecies written about in the Bible. Various countries—coincidentally, the ones who were political enemies of the United States, particularly Iran and China—were favorite tools of the devil, not to be trusted. People in the congregation confidently nodded their heads in agreement. "Amen!" they called out after each apocalyptic statement, agreeing with everything the speaker was saying.

And what exactly was he speaking? Xenophobia, racism, and fear.

I slowly slunk down in my seat, praying that nobody in the congregation was a first-time visitor, especially if they happened to be Chinese or Iranian. I realized my wife and I were a minority within this community. Our worldview was completely different from that of the hundreds of parishioners who sat around us.

This form of Christianity is fueled by a lust for power and the fear of losing it. For those used to living out their faith through the structures of Christendom, any changes that threaten their political, cultural, and societal leverage are often interpreted as spiritual threats. This is how people can rationalize their partisan politics as being Christian, how they can support depraved politicians and policies without once questioning whether they're actually endorsing something Christlike. When Roy Moore ran for Alabama's U.S. Senate seat in 2017, he faced multiple sexual misconduct allegations. He referred to the slavery era as a time when America was great. And still, 80 percent of white evangelical voters in the state supported him.[1]

Which brings us to one of the central questions facing Christians in the United States and Canada: What do we expect to "get" when we sign up to follow Jesus? Our expectations shape our experience of Christianity. Christians can get lost at both ends of the expectation spectrum: expecting prosperity and power with regard to their own lives, and expecting nothing good for the future with regard to the rest of the world. Let's look first at the great expectations that many contemporary Christians have for what their faith will bring them.

UNFULFILLED EXPECTATIONS AND MISCONCEPTIONS

To survive the spiritual journey of Christianity, you must understand what you're getting yourself into, because following Jesus will likely be harder than you imagine and more grueling than you've been told. Jesus forewarns us about the commitment: "If anyone would come after me, let him deny himself and take up his cross and follow me" (Matthew 16:24). Dedicating your life to Christ is radically different from how many pastors portray it, contradictory to how many Christians practice it, and incompatible with what many institutions claim it to be.

Many new Christians find the reality of faith to be a shocking letdown from the false premises—and promises—given to them by pastors, churches, and other believers. Spiritual expectations preface either disappointment or fulfillment, and what you were originally led to believe about the Christian faith can have significant ramifications for how you view it later in life. It's wise to evaluate what spiritual guarantees were offered to you. Before people give their lives to Christ and commit to regularly attending a church and diving headfirst into the Jesus movement, it's important to ask: What are people expecting to get out of Christianity? And more importantly, what are we selling?

WHAT DO YOU EXPECT?

People who want to follow Jesus will enter Christianity with different expectations than those who want to join Christendom. Someone who joins a Christian faith community to feed her soul and deepen her understanding of God will have a different approach than the person who joins to garner political support for the upcoming election. A person who wants to selflessly serve the poor will treat church differently than someone who owns a car dealership and knows that being seen as an upstanding Christian will be good for business. The benefits and outcomes we anticipate from our spiritual commitment will shape the identity of our faith.

This cannot be overstated. The earliest Christ-followers expected persecution and even death. They believed that someday their faith would require them to die, and they knew full well they would probably die under the most excruciating circumstances. Ironically, this actually made it *easier* for them to defend the oppressed. Facing social ridicule for belonging to a band of rejects paled in comparison with what they expected was coming.

Now contrast that idea with the modern Western expectation of going to church: entering a powerful majority culture that is privileged to hold political clout, military might, social popularity, and mainstream acceptance. In the United States and Canada, the Christian faith is often one of comfort and prosperity. Instead of becoming one of the marginalized when you join Christendom, you become one of the most powerful. For people living within Christendom, violent persecution and death for the sake of one's faith is virtually unheard of, other than in dispatches from persecuted Christians in other places around the world.

Christians living within Christendom—at least if they are white and middle class—can largely expect a safe and pleasurable life, one of assimilation into the dominant culture. It's only after we feel confident enough in our entitlement that we're moved to spare a little time, energy, and money for those in need—for those Jesus told us to love as we love ourselves. Jesus calls us to "love your enemies, and do good, and lend, expecting nothing in return" (Luke 6:35). But Christendom presents the alluring illusion that faith will make us powerful and secure. It's a tempting lie to accept, because it makes us, instead of others, the focal point.

Eventually, a church that is self-preserving rather than self-sacrificial becomes godless. Eventually, people will tire of not finding God, so they will leave the faith and look elsewhere.

EXPECTING THE WORST WHILE GLORIFYING THE PAST

Christians who don't expect the best out of their faith often expect the worst out of society. Like the apocalyptic elder who preached at my relative's church, many Christians assume they're living in the end times, with Christianity itself facing a life-and-death struggle. The problem with this view is that it regularly assumes that the present and the future are and will be much worse than the past. People who imagine that the state of Christianity is in a death spiral exaggerate both the "wholesomeness" of yesterday and the "sinfulness" of today.

Since Christendom depends on carnal power, its adherents are constantly in battle mode. But instead of being aware of spiritual warfare, in which the love of God is warring against the forces of evil, believers in Christendom fight for earthly rewards in the culture wars—votes, laws, and Supreme Court justices. And it's true: within this ongoing earthly conflict, there are signs that Christendom might be weakening. With only 55 percent of Americans actively involved in a church and Christianity's cultural dominance somewhat weakened, many Christians are experiencing an existential crisis of sorts.[2] If you think that Christianity and Christendom are the same thing, you're bound to feel threatened when Christian power begins to wane.

It's also true that at one time more people attended church on a weekly basis and officially called themselves Christians than do so now. But this period of widespread religiosity occurred during the exact same eras in which black people were ruthlessly enslaved, lynched, and terrorized; mobsters used violence to rule entire cities; women weren't allowed to vote; and Japanese Americans were forced into internment camps. During eras of rampant white supremacy, bigotry, unlawful incarceration, violence, gender inequality, corruption, human-made environmental disasters, and other abominations on a scale almost too horrific to admit—during these eras, it was somehow possible for societies to be largely considered "Christian."

Indeed, during the times in which Americans most identified as being Christian, Christian culture may have been prevalent, but following Jesus wasn't. For example, in 1948, nearly 91 percent of people in the United States identified as Christian. This was also a time in which interracial marriage was illegal, segregation was legal, and major civil rights reforms were still decades away.[3]

Don't miss this fact: during an era when churches, church attendance, and Christian institutions were at their peak, the very spirit of Christ at a societal level was largely absent. When the "Christian" empire was at the height of its national power, the spiritual state of the nation was deeply mired in the sin of racism and xenophobia. Life in the 1940s and 1950s may have been good for white, middle- and upper-class Protestant men; for everyone else, not so much. This era alone proves that even if Christians were to control what was taught in schools, legislate laws, run the government, and turn our nation back into a "Christian" society, it would all be meaningless without Jesus.

Revisionists explain away this dichotomy by suggesting that Christians who lived in those eras cannot be judged according to modern standards of morality. But such examples point clearly to the fact that Christianity can be a tool for destruction and oppression and that some Christians will do just about anything to protect the reputation of the faith. Some try to temper the severity of previous actions and to rationalize the past by saying things like "You can't judge slaveholders for participating in what was considered common at that time, because every race of people around the globe participated in the trade of humans" or "It was standard practice for medieval armies to eradicate their enemies after a battle, so Christian crusaders who annihilated entire populations were just following a cultural norm."

But Christians have always had the example of Jesus as a standard to live by, despite the particularities of their own historical context. Cultural idiosyncrasies of a time period or geographic region of the world are a poor excuse for sinful actions. What's astonishing about Jesus is that he managed to live the life he did during a time in which the Romans brutalized people and forced them to fight to the death for sheer entertainment value. If you think living a Jesus-type lifestyle is radical now, just imagine how countercultural it was back then.

After the death and resurrection of Christ, ordinary people like you and me joined a movement to follow his example. They refused to participate in societal patterns that degraded women, enslaved others, and murdered their enemies. Within a Roman Empire that ruthlessly dominated its subjects, Christians from all segments of society embraced Jesus' way of loving others—often to the point of being persecuted and killed. And if the apostle Stephen, while literally being stoned to death, could use his very last breaths to utter "Lord, do not hold this sin against them" (Acts 7:60), then those who follow Jesus and face lesser costs can make difficult choices too. So there aren't any excuses for Christians who have participated in any number of sinister movements throughout history. The example of Jesus—and his followers—was there for them to see and follow all along.

Throughout history you can also find pockets of believers who actually got it *right*—who emulated the life of Jesus against all the odds and despite everyone around them. While large portions of Christians were deluded by the Nazis' propaganda, some Jesus-followers like Magda and André Trocmé bravely stood against evil and took Jewish children into their homes at great peril to themselves. And when most of America embraced slavery, countless enslaved Christians and a few white abolitionists tirelessly fought for freedom.

Just because a majority of Christians believe something to be either good or bad or true or false doesn't mean it actually is. The ultimate litmus test for how we should live is the example of Christ—sacrificially loving others. Throughout all of time and history, doing this has never proven to be wrong. Sacrificial love has created some of the most inspirational change the world has ever seen.

One of the greatest dangers of being immersed in Christian culture is fooling ourselves into believing we're being Christian when in reality we're not. Some of the despicable atrocities mentioned above—along with countless others—are still happening today. While it's convenient to complain that our culture is becoming less Christian, we surely can't pretend that we were ever a "Christian society" to begin with.

The loss of "Christian" dominance is really good news for followers of Jesus. That sentence might seem surprising, but it's true. Although institutionalized Christianity is waning, millions are still yearning for—and genuinely believe in—God. My personal relationship with God has always been more life-giving than my relationship with religion. But for the religious leaders and gatekeepers of Christendom, the two things—institutionalized Christianity and a belief in God—cannot be separated, and many Christians are distraught about the decline of their religion's influence and power.

In fact, the death of Christendom may actually jump-start a revival of Christianity. Now more than ever, we who follow Christ have an opportunity to reflect Christ to our culture. We won't do this by trying to instill our own power structures or by trying to rebuild the fallen empire of Christendom. Rather, we will reflect Jesus by obeying his instruction to give up our power for the benefit of others. Forsake your privilege, give of your possessions, and sacrifice your comfort for the benefit of those around you. The only spiritual hope we have moving forward is valuing the person of Jesus instead of the organized religion that pretends to represent him.

So before buying into the hype that we're living in the end times, or that the world is going to hell, or that our society is becoming more depraved with each passing second, let's remember that the past wasn't better than the present. For the many communities and segments of society that have been oppressed, the past was a nightmare. And as bad as the present might be, let's entrust our future hope to nothing less than Jesus Christ.

PAYING ATTENTION TO THE MAJORITY WORLD

The belief that our society is continuously sliding deeper into moral depravity also fails to notice that in many parts of the world, the authentic message of Christ is spreading with stunning speed. While it's easy to bemoan the state of Christianity as it relates to the United States and Canada, the good news of Jesus is being shared at unprecedented rates around the globe. Miraculous revivals are occurring. Indeed, Western Christianity's preoccupation with the end times and the decline of faith makes little sense in the majority world, where millions have wholeheartedly embraced a newfound belief in Jesus and churches are experiencing unprecedented growth.

For example, in 1949 there were approximately 1 million Christians in China. In 2010 there were nearly 60 million, and some are estimating that thanks to expanding interest and growth among Christian communities, the number will reach to 160 million by 2025. By 2030, that number could be nearly 250 million people.[4] It's projected that sub-Saharan Africa will see significant growth in its Christian population as well.[5]

While these movements will possibly be plagued by the co-opting of government agendas, violence, the prosperity gospel, fundamentalism, and other entrapments, there can be no denying that a real and palpable spiritual awakening is happening. People are being freed. The oppressed are being empowered. The poor are being uplifted. Equity, justice, and hope are thriving throughout world, and in many circumstances, it's the message of Jesus that is bringing about these wonderful things.

Yet back in North America, many Christians say the state of Christianity has never been worse, and they prophesy that the rapture is imminent. In doing this, they're simplistically judging the state of the world according to how things look from a small and ethnocentric perspective. What could we learn from Christians in the majority world? A constant spiritual battle between righteousness and evil is being waged, yes. But we must always guard against hopelessness and despair. As long as Christ lives, hope endures.

THE ULTIMATE DANGER OF PESSIMISM

While pessimism is a favorite pastime for me and other Christians (God help us!), a fatalistic attitude is counterproductive to everything the gospel stands for. For Christ's sake, we can rejoice in the hope we have in God, whose promises never fail and whose blessings never cease. It's good to be reminded, "Yours, O Lord, is the greatness and the power and the glory and the victory and the majesty, for all that is in the heavens and in the earth is yours" (1 Chronicles 29:11). Having a gloomy attitude toward the world is not only counter-gospel; it's incompatible with God's omnipotence.

If you assume the worst about the future, you're denying the hope we have in Christ. Ultimately, believing that a society is without God assumes that God is not powerful enough to change hearts and minds and that God has simply given up on humanity. This not only gives an inordinate amount of influence to secularism, to the point of insinuating that it will defeat the divine love of God; it is also predicated on the idea that God is not strong enough to thwart mainstream culture.

Fatalism also gives us an excuse to be complacent about pursuing justice. Why would we try to change anything if we believe that things will inevitably get worse and that decline is actually necessary for bringing about the end of time? Such a fatalistic faith gives up on God and rejects the promises of Scripture, which show God's radical power and miraculous capacity to do good.

The Creator still lives, the Holy Spirit still lives, and Jesus still lives. The triune God is still supernaturally working in our world, and we must never succumb to the idea that the world is a lost cause. The gospel gives us an "eschatology of hope," writes Brian Zahnd. By that he means

> a Christian vision for the future that is redemptive and not destructive—more anticipating the New Jerusalem and less obsessed with Armageddon. In our anxiety-ridden world, who can doubt that we desperately need an eschatology of hope? But in order to claim that our Christian message is

"good news," we must honestly believe that we are headed for something that is ultimately hopeful. Christian happiness is based in the conviction that because of the accomplishments of Christ, the future is a friend. Without an anticipated end that justifies God's act of creation itself, happiness is mostly a form of escapist fantasy.[6]

Those of us inclined to be pessimistic about the future of Christianity, whatever our reasons, can start being optimistic about the future of Christ—who is the same yesterday, today, and forever (Hebrews 13:8). This hope can inspire us to lovingly help those around us, knowing that with God, no matter how entrenched any systemic evil may be, positive change is possible.

So the next time you hear someone grieve about the future of Christianity, remind yourself that the next generation of believers might be the most Christlike the world has ever seen. The next time you hear someone grumble about Christianity not being as good as in the "good old days" of the past, remind yourself that those days never existed in the first place.

CHANGING OUR EXPECTATIONS

Despite its imperfections, Christianity continuously manifests itself through beautiful acts of selfless love. I've witnessed Christians meet people who were homeless and decide right then and there to invite them into their homes to live—and they did. I've seen lifelong addicts break drug addictions through the help of a church. I've known families without food to have groceries miraculously provided to them at just the right time. Countless individuals have told me their personal stories of how they couldn't find love or acceptance anywhere other than at their local church.

My daughter's Girl Scout troop meets in the basement of a church, and at least once a week another nearby church provides a free meal to anyone who wants one. Other local churches host fish fries and spaghetti dinners and do service projects like mowing lawns, painting homes, and cleaning up local parks. I once went into a coffee shop that was entirely subsidized by a church, and everything was free. When I tried to pay for my large double mocha, I stood dumbfounded while the cashier politely explained that all the products were gifts to the community. A church in my hometown provides emergency assistance, counseling, budgeting classes, premarital counseling, meals, drug and alcohol recovery groups, grief support groups, anxiety and depression support groups, a food pantry, a meet-up time for adults with disabilities, a job skills program, temporary shelter for the homeless, housing assistance, and a daycare for low-income families. That's just one church!

My wife is an elementary teacher, and one day she came home and told me that a random church had provided donuts for all the teachers. It turns out that the church had decided to "adopt" the elementary school, gifting supplies for the kids, clothing for students in need, and food for the teachers and staff.

Christian organizations such as Preemptive Love Coalition and Mennonite Central Committee counteract violence and provide humanitarian aid to those who desperately need it. Compassion International and World Relief have helped innumerable people receive food, education, and shelter and have transformed the lives of countless individuals. It's hard to imagine our society without the work of the Salvation Army, the YMCA, and Alcoholics Anonymous, each founded on the belief that God's love transforms people. Some statistics suggest that people of faith give more generously to charities (to both secular and religious causes), volunteer more of their time, and provide the majority of non-federal relief after natural disasters.[7] Time and again I've seen churches carry people through the very worst moments of their lives. For all the pain and suffering Christians have caused, there can be no denying that followers of Christ have done incredible good too.

When we shift our expectations of what Christianity will do for us—from expecting to *gain* power and privilege for ourselves to expecting to *give* to others—we see the true Jesus at work. And when Christians stop expecting society to free-fall into the end times and start trusting in God's promises for the future, we see Jesus glorified.

5

Why the Image
of God Matters

After this I looked, and behold, a great multitude that no one could number, from every nation, from all tribes and peoples and languages, standing before the throne and before the Lamb, clothed in white robes, with palm branches in their hands.
—REVELATION 7:9

I was born into Christendom. Specifically, I was born into American evangelical Christendom. To be even more precise, I was born in 1982, to white parents who attended a small nondenominational, charismatic church located in Saint Paul, Minnesota. Since it was America in the early 1980s, I statistically had about a 90 percent chance of being born into a family that affiliated itself with some form of Christianity. The odds were in my favor.

But what if I had been born and raised in Somalia instead? If that were the case, I would have had less than a 1 percent chance of being born into a Christian family. Almost certainly I would have grown up Muslim. Sometimes I imagine how my life would be the same or different in such a scenario. If I had been born in Somalia, would I just be an Islamic version of who I am today? As a kid, would I have participated in puppet programs at the local mosque? Would I have gotten special badges for memorizing sections of the Qur'an? Would my parents have reprimanded me for falling asleep while the imam rambled on and on in religious jargon I couldn't possibly comprehend? Would my teachers have used flannelgraph characters to tell us stories about Harut and Marut? As a teenager, would I have listened to a hip Islamic worship band? Would I have gone to Al-Azhar University and minored in Qur'an studies? Would I have become an imam instead of a youth pastor?

An infinite number of factors shape our existence and faith in unquantifiable ways. We have control over some of these things but absolutely no control over others. Why was I born into the Christian faith while others—billions of others—are born into other religions or no religion at all?

Jesus is unique: a divine God unlike any other human being. I believe this to my core. Billions of people make up Christianity, and each individual person has been shaped by trillions of circumstances—many of which are beyond one's will or choice. Christianity is too vast to fully comprehend, and I still haven't met one single follower of Christ who believes the exact same things I do, shares the exact same spiritual experiences I have had, or who has found faith in God the exact same way I did—and I never will. Yet we all love the same unchanging God. If we accept this about Christianity, we must also admit that the billions of people who live outside of Christianity have also been shaped by trillions of influences beyond their control too.

There's the temptation in Christendom to be pretentious about one's own beliefs in relation to the beliefs of non-Christians. Christians sometimes perceive people who aren't followers of Christ as less moral, less worthy. Non-Christians are "lost," "sheep gone astray," "blind," and "deceived." Christians can be downright mean and exclusionary toward outsiders. One of the legacies that Christ-followers are reckoning with is the legacy of this exclusion.

But Jesus wasn't like this at all. He went far out of his way to show everyone their worth regardless of their religion, beliefs, or actions. The promotion of Christianity should never happen through the demotion of others, and we must realize that non-Christians have their own reasons for not being a part of the Christian faith. I heartily believe in evangelism—that is, sharing the good news of Jesus (see chapter 8). But the good news of Christ is only good news if it tells the full story of a God who created all humans in the image of God.

Just as we recognize that our own faith is influenced by an array of outside influences, we must grant that the same goes for unbelievers, as well as believers with whom we disagree. The way that people see God is formulated by countless variables, both big and small. No matter how much you may clash with someone's religion or beliefs, somewhere within the unfathomable mixture of particles that make up a person's core being are valid reasons for how that person came to be.

When we follow Jesus, we extend love and mercy to everyone—including and especially those who don't. In this chapter we look at the complex interplay of factors that make us who we are. We consider the truth that the image of God dwells in each human being, which means that if we kill another human, we are killing the image of God in them. That truth changes everything.

DID WE CHOOSE CHRISTIANITY, OR DID CHRISTIANITY CHOOSE US?

At some point, most Christians ask themselves how they came to believe in Jesus. What were the determining factors? Did God supernaturally speak to you? Did Jesus reveal himself through a miracle or special revelation? How did your faith come into being? Or you may find yourself asking how your faith fizzled out or became irrelevant. Did you face a trauma that made you question God's character? Did a friend ask you questions about your faith that you'd never considered before?

Conditions beyond our own choices play huge—often determining—roles in whether we're Christians. Were you raised in a Christian home, with Christian parents, in a place where Christianity was the dominant religion? What experiences shaped your faith? Many Christians rationalize these countless influences and explain them away as God's sovereignty: "Everything was meant to happen this way, so this is why I believe in God." And while God surely did play a role in these circumstances, we must also appreciate the responsibility of other active agents: ourselves, others, the spiritual forces of both good and evil, and the laws of nature. Jumbled together, all these entities form who we are. Even the slightest of alterations could have caused us to have different beliefs, possibly rejecting (or not discovering) Christianity altogether.

Even though our actions and choices are deeply meaningful, so are the countless forces that happen outside our ability to control them. Everyone—for better or worse—has a worldview deeply dependent on variables beyond their own reckoning.

Yes, following Jesus is a choice. The apostle John states that "whoever believes in him should not perish but have eternal life" (John 3:16), and Jesus himself said, "For unless you believe that I am he you will die in your sins" (John 8:24). We should never negate the significance of choosing to follow Jesus. No external circumstances can ever take away one's personal responsibility to decide whether to love God. Nor should we ever downplay someone's belief or unbelief by suggesting it's merely a consequence of random variables. But we also must humbly recognize the validity of others' spiritual journeys. Just as God moved within our lives, we must also trust that God is gracefully moving in the lives of all people.

We must trust in the love and grace of God. Brennan Manning speaks to the power of God's grace in an impassioned section of *The Ragamuffin Gospel*:

> Because salvation is by grace through faith, I believe that among the countless number of people standing in front of the throne and in front of the Lamb, dressed in white robes and holding palms in their hands (see Revelation 7:9), I shall see the prostitute from the Kit-Kat Ranch in Carson City, Nevada, who tearfully told me that she could find no other employment to support her two-year-old son. I shall see the woman who had an abortion and is haunted by guilt and remorse but did the best she could faced with grueling alternatives; the businessman besieged with debt who sold his integrity in a series of desperate transactions; the insecure clergyman addicted to being liked, who never challenged his people from the pulpit and longed for unconditional love; the sexually abused teen molested by his father and now selling his body on the street, who, as he

falls asleep each night after his last "trick," whispers the name of the unknown God he learned about in Sunday school. . . . "But how?" we ask. Then the voice says, "They have washed their robes and have made them white in the blood of the Lamb." There they are. There *we* are—the multitude who so wanted to be faithful, who at times got defeated, soiled by life, and bested by trials, wearing the bloodied garments of life's tribulations, but through it all clung to faith. My friends, if this is not good news to you, you have never understood the gospel of grace.[1]

WIDENING THE STREAM OF INFLUENCES

My knowledge of Christianity was largely formulated at the feet of people who were white, male, and American. Almost my entire understanding of God was made up of these three single factors: white, male, American. If you were to create a pie chart of all Christians in the world, white American males make up only a slight percentage, yet my spirituality was disproportionately influenced by them. The pastors who preached the sermons, the professors at my Bible college, the authors of the devotionals I read, the writers of the textbooks I studied, the theologians I admired, my mentors and role models—almost all were white American men. I learned about gender roles from white American men. I learned about race from white American men. I learned about politics from white American men. I learned about theology from white American men. I learned about Jesus from white American men.

We can all be guilty of restricting our spiritual influences to the voices that most closely match our own. We need to fervently guard ourselves from turning God into an ethnocentric entity—especially one who favors our own preferred culture over the cultures of others.

It was during this time—when I was limiting influences to people who looked like me—that I was the most convinced that I understood Christianity better than anyone else. I was living in a spiritual bubble. Frankly, it's heartbreaking to look back and see how narrow my faith was. I would need to unlearn, relearn, and keep learning from people who weren't white, who weren't men, who weren't American—people who weren't like me. Christianity requires perpetual learning, and it requires teachers who are different from us—especially people who are on the margins.

PENTECOST

When the Holy Spirit arrived and descended on the early followers of Jesus, hierarchies were shaken up and social divides were spanned.

> On the day of Pentecost all the believers were meeting together in one place. Suddenly, there was a sound from heaven like the roaring of a mighty windstorm, and it filled the house where they were sitting. Then, what looked like flames or tongues of fire appeared and settled on each of them. And everyone present was filled with the Holy Spirit and began speaking in other languages, as the Holy Spirit gave them this ability.
>
> At that time there were devout Jews from every nation living in Jerusalem. When they heard the loud noise, everyone came running, and they were bewildered to hear their own languages being spoken by the believers.
>
> They were completely amazed. "How can this be?" they exclaimed. "These people are all from Galilee, and yet we hear them speaking in our own native languages! Here we are—Parthians, Medes, Elamites, people from Mesopotamia, Judea, Cappadocia, Pontus, the province of Asia, Phrygia,

Pamphylia, Egypt, and the areas of Libya around Cyrene, visitors from Rome (both Jews and converts to Judaism), Cretans, and Arabs. And we all hear these people speaking in our own languages about the wonderful things God has done!" They stood there amazed and perplexed. "What can this mean?" they asked each other. (Act 2:1-12 NLT)

Pentecost was the vital moment in which the very Spirit of God was given as a gift to empower believers. But what's commonly overlooked is that this defining moment of Christianity was a miracle allowing people to understand each other despite their different languages, ethnicities, and cultural backgrounds. This was the Holy Spirit's very first task on the job: *connecting people who were different from each other.*

It's no coincidence that after the arrival of the Holy Spirit, followers of Jesus were divinely inspired to go out into the world and preach the good news of the gospel. They were suddenly driven to love and sacrificially serve those who weren't anything like them—to resolve conflicts they had with others, to see beyond their self-centeredness, and to challenge their biases. Christianity was no longer a "this is ours" thing to be hoarded and protected; it became a "this is for you" hope to be celebrated and shared.

Instead of launching a crusade meant to overtake and subdue communities through violence and control, the Spirit of God used the transformational power of love across racial, social, gender, and ethnic boundaries. It wasn't a campaign to destroy different cultures or to degrade people according to their societal classification. It was a liberating movement to bless everyone.

Loving those who are different from you—working to empower those who look, act, and think differently than you do—is a sign of the Holy Spirit. Jesus proclaimed, "A new commandment I give to you, that you love one another: just as I have loved you, you also are to love one another" (John 13:34). If you're ever confused about what to do in any given situation, do whatever is the most loving.

Oppressing others is incompatible with following God. The Bible instructs us to "love one another, for love is from God, and whoever loves has been born of God and knows God. Anyone who does not love does not know God, because God is love" (1 John 4:7-8). To degrade anyone because they're different from you is to oppose the Holy Spirit, to directly oppose God. Scripture goes on to say, "Those who say, 'I love God,' and hate their brothers or sisters, are liars; for those who do not love a brother or sister whom they have seen, cannot love God whom they have not seen. The commandment we have from him is this: those who love God must love their brothers and sisters also" (1 John 4:20-21 NRSV).

In Jesus' time, the spiritual rulers preferred the age-old systems of separation and caste based on legalism and fallible human perceptions of value. They wanted to lord over others and have power over them. But then Jesus came along and turned everything upside down. He proclaimed that the first shall be last (Matthew 20:16). Mary, his mother, declared that the rich shall be sent away empty and the hungry will be filled (Luke 1:53). The apostle Paul said that there will be neither Jew nor Gentile, neither male nor female (Galatians 3:28). All will be united in Christ! Jesus was ridiculed and eventually killed on the cross for spreading such sentiments.

Unfortunately, they remain just as unpopular today as they were back then.

IMAGO DEI

As Genesis 1:27 declares, everyone is created in the image of God. Everyone—including non-Christians. Every person bears the *imago Dei* (the image of God) within. Let that sink in for a moment.

If you really want to radically change the way you see and value others, start practicing the belief that everyone is made in the image of God. The biblical definition of a human being is an individual loved by God and created in God's divine image. Your boss: an individual loved by God and created in God's divine image. Your political opponent: an individual loved by God and created in God's divine image. The person sleeping in the alley: an individual loved by God and created in God's divine image. A terrorist: an individual loved by God and created in God's divine image.

The fact that everyone has divine worth is why Christians should pause before acting against him, her, them, Muslims, North Koreans, terrorists, and other human beings to whom we ascribe generic adjectives in order to deny their Christlikeness. Before we go to war with our enemies, we should ask ourselves, "Can we go to war against these individuals created in God's divine image?" Before we scream at somebody in a fit of rage, we should ask ourselves, "Should I swear against this individual, who is loved by God and created in God's divine image?"

The truth that people are passionately loved by God and created in God's image changes the way we view humanity. It transforms our attitudes and beliefs. This is one of the reasons Jesus always chose love and nonviolence: he would never hurt or destroy someone he loves.

Think of a person, or various people, whom you absolutely love. Imagine this love you have for them. Take a few moments to vividly picture it in your mind. This love is real, meaningful, and vital to you. This is how God feels about every single person on earth. And this is why God is so adamant that we love each other, that we love our neighbor as we love ourselves, that we love even our enemies. When we hurt others, we're hurting family. When we kill others, we're killing family.

Christians have a hard time grasping this truth. But looking at Jesus, we discover that we cannot deny the centrality of loving our enemy:

> And one of the scribes came up and heard them disputing with one another, and seeing that he answered them well, asked him, "Which commandment is the most important of all?" Jesus answered, "The most important is, 'Hear, O Israel: The Lord our God, the Lord is one. And you shall love the Lord your God with all your heart and with all your soul and with all your mind and with all your strength.' The second is this: 'You shall love your neighbor as yourself.' There is no other commandment greater than these." And the scribe said to him, "You are right, Teacher. You have truly said that he is one, and there is no other besides him." (Mark 12:28-32)

> But I say to you who hear, Love your enemies, do good to those who hate you. (Luke 6:27)

In his book *Drop the Stones*, author Carlos Rodríguez writes:

> Saving the adulterous woman from being brutally killed was an act of justice on the part of Jesus. We know that to the "God-specialists," it would have been lawful to disfigure her to death, but to God, it was ungodly. The woman caught in the act of adultery was the *Imago Dei*, the image of God on earth—created in His likeness, designed for inheritance, and worthy of justice. Just like everyone else.

100% of women of color were created in God's image.

100% of radical Muslims were created in God's image.

100% of undocumented immigrants were created in God's image.

All 100% of you were created as the *Imago Dei.*[2]

Understanding that everyone is lovingly created in God's image is the only way the radical lifestyle that Jesus lived makes any sense. It's why he didn't retaliate when he was unjustly arrested. It's why he didn't ruthlessly destroy his enemies. It's why he didn't return hate with hate. It's why he didn't call down a legion of angels to do his bidding. The people Jesus saw and interacted with were his family: people and individuals he loved desperately and beyond our ability to comprehend. And when these beloved people turned on him, tortured him, and mocked him, and as his body hung limply from a cross and succumbed to death, Jesus gathered the very last of his strength to utter, "Father, forgive them, for they know not what they do" (Luke 23:34).

Love your enemies? *Forgive* them? By today's standards, these actions may seem absurd and illogical. But the Holy Spirit can help us see others in the same way Christ sees them. It's almost as if God knew that the example of Jesus wouldn't be enough to convince us, knew that we might write off the story of Jesus by saying, "Well, but Jesus is God and we are not!" Shortly after the descriptions of Jesus' crucifixion, we are given an account of the very first Christian martyr, Stephen, who faithfully emulated Christ and, like Jesus, was the victim of persecution and violence. Seized by religious leaders, Stephen was also unfairly tried and set upon by an angry mob. As Stephen was being stoned to death, instead of responding in hate or bitterness, he too used his very last breaths to utter these final words: "Lord, do not hold this sin against them" (Acts 7:60).

Humans have a distinct honor in being loved by God and created in God's divine image. Not even the angels are said to be created in God's image—only we have this special designation of being the *imago Dei*. But before you can recognize that everyone is loved by God and created in God's divine image, you must first accept the fact that *you* are loved by God and created in God's divine image. You are divinely loved, divinely created. Take some time to silently meditate on this truth. This is the profound meaning of our very existence.

A FAMILY, UNITED BUT UNIQUE

Christianity is a worldwide community of billions of people who speak different languages, value different cultural beliefs, practice different traditions, but all worship the same God. Christianity isn't an American religion. It isn't a white religion. It isn't an English-based religion. It isn't constrained—despite the efforts of many to do so—by any demographic factor, physical trait, political movement, social rank, financial status, race, culture, state, or society. For thousands of years, Jesus has transformed the lives of countless people, and if you are a follower of Jesus you are part of this legacy.

Following Jesus means being humble enough to recognize our presuppositions and brave enough to admit our stereotypes and limited perspectives. Christians are united in Christ, but this doesn't mean we should erase cultures, abandon our own culture, or become a homogeneous people who value uniform looks, behaviors, and beliefs. No, we must embrace the reality that the "Christian heritage" is as vast and assorted as the people who represent it. The book of Revelation paints this gorgeous portrait: "After this I looked, and behold, a great multitude that no one could number, from every nation, from all tribes and peoples and languages, standing before the throne and before the Lamb, clothed in white robes, with palm branches in their hands" (Revelation 7:9).

Imagine this truth: If you are a Christian, every other Christian around the world right now is your family member. These family members—your spiritual siblings—are just as connected to you as your blood relatives. Jesus himself says, "For whoever does the will of my Father in heaven is my brother and sister and mother" (Matthew 12:50). God believes this, but do we?

The apostle John writes, "But to all who did receive him, who believed in his name, he gave the right to become children of God, who were born, not of blood nor of the will of the flesh nor of the will of man, but of God" (John 1:12-13). Jesus is a significant bond that goes beyond just a random commonality. You are invested into a corporate identity and are part of the body of believers. Practice imagining the global family of God. Think of it when you watch the news and realize your family in Christ is being affected by the natural disasters, famines, wars, political machinations, and current events that are being reported on a daily basis.

Christians sometimes use the expression "sister in Christ" or "brother in Christ" to refer to another believer. These terms are deeply authentic, because Christians are a family. We really are spiritual siblings to each other. By all accounts this is a crazy family, with good and bad theologians, good and bad practices, and good and bad people. We're weird, judgmental, loving, modern, old-fashioned, young, elderly, male, female, straight, gay. Call us the most eccentric family ever. We're all imperfect people loved by a perfect God.

RECOGNIZING OUR SPIRITUAL AND CULTURAL INSULARITY

Studies show that in the United States, an individual's social network consists primarily of people of her or his own race. "People can meet God within their cultural context," writes Christena Cleveland in *Disunity in Christ*. But to *follow* God, she says, "they must cross into other cultures because that's what Jesus did in the incarnation and on the cross."[3]

Moving from an insular faith to a less biased one isn't easy, and it's a lifelong process that never ends. Early experiences of deconstructing an isolated, insulated Christianity for the sake of one lived within a diverse community will often arrive in the form of fear, conflict, and awkwardness. In his book *Culture Care*, Makoto Fujimura discusses the role of those who journey back and forth between various groups. He writes, "Life on the borders of a group—and in the space between groups—is prone to dangers literal and figurative, with people both at 'home' and among the 'other' likely to misunderstand or mistrust the motivations, piety, and loyalty of the border-stalker." Yet all this potential distress is nothing compared to the certain harm of *not* dismantling our insularity—of not seeking out the wisdom of Christians who are different from us. As Fujimura goes on to say, those who cross borders can perform "a role of cultural leadership in a new mode, serving functions including empathy, memory, warning, guidance, mediation, and reconciliation. Those who journey to the borders of their group and beyond will encounter new vistas and knowledge that can enrich the group."[4]

People who cross barriers to listen and learn, as Fujimura describes, and then return with their knowledge and communicate it to their own group should be commended. But there is also great need for caution. Using intermediaries of our own socioeconomic and ethnic groups can establish a poor precedent fraught with problems.[5] Not only is information transferred secondhand, but with every degree of separation there's an increased risk of losing authenticity and accuracy. Nuances are missed, and the narratives become simplified and can be co-opted to fit another's agenda.

Relying on go-betweens also puts the information at risk of being translated through the worldview of the communicator, where source material is curated and filtered accordingly. In many such scenarios the majority culture, or those with the most political and social power, wins out, while the voices of the oppressed are policed to fit the expectations of the privileged. "The biases we hold against other groups have the ability to wreak havoc on our crosscultural interactions," Christena Cleveland warns. "Before we enter into such interactions, we must do the difficult work of addressing our biases and blind spots."[6]

Today, it's hard to imagine any school banning interracial dating. But until the year 2000, this was the rule at the predominantly white Bob Jones University, a fundamentalist Christian school. Examples like this show that discrimination is fostered through institutional precedents, bylaws, and traditions, often cloaked in the most subtle forms. Such policies may seem innocuous to those who adhere to—and implement—them, but it is through such machinations that evil flourishes. Participants and silent observers are not going to be card-carrying KKK members or have swastikas tattooed on their bodies, yet they'll achieve the same end. Austin Channing Brown writes, "When you believe niceness disproves the presence of racism, it's easy to start believing bigotry is rare, and that the label racist should be applied only to mean-spirited, intentional acts of discrimination."[7]

Years from now, how will our generation be judged? Like addicts going through major withdrawal, who may initially despise medical staff for trying to break them free of their chemical dependency, spiritually broken people will initially dislike anyone who challenges their discriminatory faith. Any rehabilitation must begin with acknowledgment, with taking responsibility. The process is hard. But we grow more mature by learning profound truths from Christian communities beyond our own.

One method of gaining this knowledge is to imagine information as being received through a window. If your spiritual learning and experiences are within environments that consist of people who look like you, believe the same things as you, and share most of your demographic and cultural traits, you're looking into a mirror. But if it's received from someone who doesn't share the majority of your perspectives, who is notably different from you, you're looking through a window. Seeking and receiving information through windows and not just mirrors is especially critical for people in dominant cultures.

Theologian Grace Ji-Sun Kim offers four helpful steps for Christians struggling to embrace those who are different from them:

1. Overcome the doubt as to whether Jesus really wanted us to embrace the Other.

2. Overcome the fear of the unknown. We are afraid to embrace those who are different from us . . .

3. Spend the energy, time, and commitment to embrace people. Embracing is not a verbal proclamation. It's not a simple act of getting to know another. It requires patient and persistent love.

4. We need to open ourselves to the Spirit who moves within us to move us to embrace those who are different from us, to embrace the Other.[8]

As Christians, we must create more windows to the world beyond us.[9] But doing this requires following Jesus, which is not always the easiest or most comfortable choice.

How to Avoid Following Jesus

Do not be conformed to this world, but be transformed by the renewal of your mind, that by testing you may discern what is the will of God, what is good and acceptable and perfect.
—ROMANS 12:2

Every weekday I wake up and get ready for my job that earns me an annual salary close to $10,000 less than the average recent college grad.

I'm in my thirties.

After showering, brushing my teeth, and eating a quick breakfast, I put on one of the two pairs of dress pants that I own (each given to me secondhand), then one of four dress shirts (also secondhand). After that I throw on a scuffed-up pair of dress shoes, kiss my family goodbye, and go out to my car.

My car is a '98 Honda Civic. A junker. Rust chunks fall off every time I open or shut the door. The front end is damaged from the time my mother-in-law accidentally backed into it. The wipers are broken, the body is covered in a film of dirt and road salt, and it makes all sorts of noises depending on whether you stop, start, accelerate, slow down, or simply coast. Sometimes it even makes noises when the engine isn't running.

As I drive to work, I spend most of my time on a busy highway stuck in traffic, listening to the few channels my radio can pick up, and daydreaming about how my life could be better. The air conditioning is broken, and the heater only works when the fan is on high, so the comfort level is largely dependent on my speed and how far I roll down the windows. And rolling down the windows helps, since my car smells like old diapers and dead leaves, mostly thanks to the sticks and dirt stuck in my center console from the time my kids decided to turn my car into a mobile compost bin. I watch as almost every car that passes mine is cleaner, shinier, newer, and vastly more expensive. I drive past neighborhoods with houses ten times bigger than mine. I observe drivers as they talk on fancier smartphones, sip craft espresso drinks, wear brand-name sunglasses, and head off to their lucrative corporate jobs.

Upon arriving at work, I go to my desk and begin my entry-level job. First I catch up on emails from my bosses, most of whom are younger than I am. During breaks at work I sometimes browse social media, envying friends who are clearly richer, healthier, more successful, and more attractive than I am.

Maybe you catch yourself living with this type of mindset: being self-conscious of your status in society. But comparing myself to others and analyzing my worth according to impossible standards is not only unhealthy; it's counterintuitive to the gospel of Jesus. The apostle Peter proclaims that we are "a chosen race, a royal priesthood, a holy nation, a people for his own possession, that you may proclaim the excellencies of him who called you out of darkness into his marvelous light" (1 Peter 2:9).

The surrounding culture is constantly influencing us and shaping our identity. We're born into this tense reality, and before we can even think for ourselves, we're being shaped by cultural influences. What we choose to do with those influences—accept or resist or transform them—matters.

When Jesus died on the cross, his disciples didn't become famous, they didn't gain financial wealth, they didn't acquire political influence, they didn't obtain power, and they didn't become comfortable. Following Jesus meant the exact opposite. They would sacrifice it all, living a life filled with persecution, pain, and suffering. Most would end up being viciously murdered—martyred—for the sake of following this Prince of Peace. By being Christ-followers, they were endangering everyone around them: their friends, family, and loved ones. They were literally giving up everything. The earliest Christians were killed in the most gruesome and horrific circumstances: tortured, burned alive, crucified on crosses, fed to lions and beasts, and killed in the most sadistic ways possible. Committing oneself to Christ really meant giving away your life.

So how did Christianity become so obsessed with wealth and so bent on self-preservation? It's a question Christians must honestly ask themselves. Are we serving *the least of these*, or are we serving ourselves? Are we following Jesus, or are we following other Christians? Are we committed to Jesus, or are we avoiding him?

In this chapter we look at ways that we as Christians often avoid following Jesus. Examining several ways that we commonly avoid following Jesus might help us learn authentic ways to follow him.

FIND AN IDENTITY IN CONSUMPTION RATHER THAN CHRIST

Your coworker is a diehard fan of the Green Bay Packers. Your uncle is obsessed with the Beatles. Your friend is a sci-fi cosplay enthusiast, and your neighbor is known for her affinity for Tesla automobiles. Chances are that you, too, are known by a subculture with which you identify. Chances are that your identity is linked to the products you choose to consume.

We are constantly being targeted as potential consumers. In almost every area of our lives, companies vie for our attention and purchase of their products and services and allegiance to their brands. The average person now spends about five hours on a mobile device and close to ten hours a day consuming media (including television, radio, Internet, magazines, and newspapers). During this time they will view hundreds of ads.[1] This perpetual onslaught can significantly affect where we invest our time and energy. Spending countless hours playing video games, binge-watching our favorite television shows, supporting our favorite sports teams, and devoting ourselves to a particular activity or hobby combine to create our identities as consumers.

Many of us feel a real sense of anxiety associated with constantly having to choose, with always being put in a position of picking between competing products and navigating through the constant rhetoric and propaganda.

The sheer volume and intensity of living within such a climate is tiring. It can feel as if we have no space left in our lives

for anything more—including God. The choices are burden-
some, and even when we try our best it can seem as if nothing
is ever good enough. No matter what decisions we make, or
even if we attempt to avoid societal expectations altogether,
we can still feel guilty, unworthy, and even alienated.

We've been trained by our culture to find our identities in
everything but Christ. We've been trained to care only for ourselves and our families.

SUPPORT A CULTURE OF DEATH

Christianity is built on the premise that Christ defeated
death. But many Christians in the United States and Canada
support death-dealing ways rather than life-giving ones. To be
a Christian is to bring about life, not snuff it out. Dominant
Christianity, however, has largely committed itself to powers
that prefer annihilation over restoration. Christians—people
who claim to follow a God who created and loves everyone—
are often the most adamant that people sometimes need to kill
other people.

If you were to read the Bible without any previous Christian influence, you would find an amazing drama that climaxes
with the death and resurrection of Jesus. Regardless of your
favorite chapter or story, you would know it is a narrative
that revolves around Jesus. Now consider today's dominant
Christian culture and how it is so *unlike* Jesus—particularly
as it relates to violence and death. If you believe that Jesus is
accurately portrayed in Scripture, you know beyond a shadow
of a doubt that he was radically peaceful and nonviolent. He
defeated death to bring about life. This is why he saved people
from death, literally raised them from the dead, to bring about
life. He never once killed anyone or participated in violence or

any act that would endanger or take away human life—despite having legions of angels at his disposal and the indestructible power to kill any enemy within his grasp.

Killing goes against Christ's very nature of bringing life. When you carry a sidearm, or support warfare, or vote for the death penalty, you are declaring that you are okay with killing a creation of God—okay with destroying someone whom God knows and loves. So how did Christians—especially certain groups of them—gain a reputation for being pro-war, pro-gun, pro-capital punishment, and pro-death?

Guns.

Over half of white evangelicals in the United States own guns. Historically, white evangelicals have stood out as being one of the only religious groups consistently opposed to increased gun restrictions.[2] While speaking about the 2015 shooting in San Bernardino, California, Jerry Falwell Jr., president of one of the nation's largest Christian universities, remarked: "If more good people had concealed-carry permits, then we could end those Muslims before they walked in and killed them. . . . Let's teach them a lesson if they ever show up here."[3] Compare that to what Jesus says in Luke 6:27-31: "But I say to you who hear, Love your enemies, do good to those who hate you, bless those who curse you, pray for those who abuse you. To one who strikes you on the cheek, offer the other also, and from one who takes away your cloak do not withhold your tunic either. Give to everyone who begs from you, and from one who takes away your goods do not demand them back. And as you wish that others would do to you, do so to them."

In 2015, roughly 13,000 people were killed by guns in the United States.[4] Globally, about 500,000 people die from gun violence every year.[5] That's half a million people. While Christians in the United States should be concerned about gun violence in their own country, they should also be alarmed that the United States is responsible for many of the gun deaths that happen beyond its borders. According to a recent report, the United States is the leading producer of small arms, exporting billions of dollars' worth of small arms into the world.[6]

Few people have captured America's gun culture better than author Gary Younge, whose book *Another Day in the Death of America* describes a typical day in the United States: "It was just another day in America. And as befits an unremarkable Saturday in America, ten children and teens were killed by gunfire. Like the weather that day, none of them would make big news beyond their immediate locale, because, like the weather, their deaths did not intrude on the accepted order of things but conformed to it. So in terms of what one might expect of a Saturday in America, there wasn't a hint of 'betrayal' about this either; it's precisely the tally the nation has come to expect."[7]

Christians who support the use of guns often do so under the premise of fearmongering rhetoric about terrorism, personal safety, apocalyptic end times, and imminent war. They allow dread and suspicion to supersede the desire to follow Christ's gospel teachings of sacrificially loving others. It's as if they don't trust that God is able to protect them.

War.

The United States and many of the businesses within it profit from weapons sales and exports. There are executives, some of whom claim the name of Christ, whose success is determined by how effective their products are at killing people.

Think about that for a moment. Profits, stocks, and quarterly reports are dependent on the blood of others—and how efficiently it can be spilled. Even in an age of drones and high-tech weaponry capable of mass destruction, a whopping 60 to 90 percent of deaths in military conflicts are caused by small arms and light weapons.[8] This means that most deaths are the result of somebody taking a gun, aiming it, and pulling the trigger—eliminating a life created in God's image. And doing this is essential to keeping businesses successful.

Christians in the United States haven't exactly followed the Prince of Peace when it comes to loving our enemies. At the beginning of 2003, 77 percent of Christians supported the Iraq War.[9] Although some Christian denominations and communities issued strong statements denouncing the war, conspicuously absent from these groups were a majority of American Christians.[10]

In 2010, while discussing the United State's involvement in Afghanistan, Leith Anderson, president of the National Association of Evangelicals, said this: "Most evangelicals in America subscribe to the theological position called 'Just War Theory,' that it is morally justifiable to go to war under certain conditions. The problem with Afghanistan is that the nature of the war is so complex that it is difficult to know whether this falls within the confines of a just war."[11]

It's this "complexity" that many present-day Christians are understandably having a hard time reconciling with their faith—a faith that demands nonviolence in even the most illogical of scenarios. Take, for example, the disciple Peter, who drew his own sword in an attempt to defend Jesus from being unjustly arrested. If anybody had a reasonable and justifiable defense, it's Peter, right? He was defending an innocent man—who also happened to be God—from blatant evil. And yet Jesus condemned Peter!

Jesus could have called on angels to wipe out his enemies. He could have saved himself. Soldiers are brave to face bullets and the possibility of death, but they're also abiding by the cultural norm of hitting back. The most insanely brave act a person can do is to nonviolently love an enemy—even in the face of death. Even our enemies are loved by God. Think about the person—or people—you hate and despise most in your life. Now realize that they are divinely created in the image of God.

Following Jesus may seem completely illogical. But it's within this counterintuitive love that the holy nature of God is fully revealed.

The death penalty.

More than 70 percent of evangelical Christians support the death penalty. That's the largest proportion of any religious group.[12]

There are hopeful signs that evangelicals may be changing their pro-death views. Between 2011 and 2015, there was a 6 percent drop in evangelicals' support for capital punishment, and in 2015 the National Association of Evangelicals passed a resolution that backed down from its previously strong support of the death penalty.[13] And more and more evangelical leaders are speaking out against gun violence and the death-dealing power of the National Rifle Association.

Christians like Shane Claiborne continually advocate against the death penalty. In his book *Executing Grace*, Claiborne writes:

> Capital punishment offers us one version of justice. There is a sensibility to it: evil should not go without consequence. And there is a theology behind it: "An eye for an eye . . . a tooth for tooth." Yet grace offers us another version of

justice. Grace makes room for redemption. Grace offers us a vision for justice that is restorative, and dedicated to healing the wounds of injustice. But the grace thing is hard work. It takes faith—because it dares us to believe that not only can victims be healed, but so can the victimizers. It is not always easy to believe that love is more powerful than hatred, life more powerful than death, and that people can be better than the worst thing they've done. These two versions of justice compete for our allegiance. One leads to death. The other can lead to life.[14]

We must be careful not to assume that Christians are *intentionally* pro-death. Most Christians in the United States believe that abortion is immoral. In the United States, hundreds of thousands of abortions occur each year.[15] For these Christians, many of whom are also against the death penalty and war and who support gun control, there may seem to be few options for affiliating with a political party. The issues about which they care deeply are "owned" by opposing political parties. The abortion debate is always far more nuanced than people across the political spectrum like to admit. For Christians who vote, this is a complex moral quandary.

Finding common cause around life-giving rather than death-dealing is a large task before us. Removing our support for the culture of death will be long and hard. Keeping Christ central will be key.

IGNORE THE LEAST OF THESE

Being immersed in a Western cultural existence has shaped our priorities as Christians. Dominant Christian culture has become more passionate about electing officials into office than rescuing refugees, and more adamant about protecting the stock market than helping immigrants. Time and again, we've prioritized our own worldly gains over the well-being of others. The likelihood of Christians facing any substantial consequences on earth for doing this is small, but the Bible says we will have to answer to God. There will be a reckoning. Matthew 25:31-46 says,

> When the Son of Man comes in his glory, and all the angels with him, then he will sit on his glorious throne. Before him will be gathered all the nations, and he will separate people one from another as a shepherd separates the sheep from the goats. And he will place the sheep on his right, but the goats on the left. Then the King will say to those on his right, "Come, you who are blessed by my Father, inherit the kingdom prepared for you from the foundation of the world. For I was hungry and you gave me food, I was thirsty and you gave me drink, I was a stranger and you welcomed me, I was naked and you clothed me, I was sick and you visited me, I was in prison and you came to me." Then the righteous will answer him, saying, "Lord, when did we see you hungry and feed you, or thirsty and give you drink? And when did we see you a stranger and welcome you, or naked and clothe you? And when did we see you sick or in prison and visit you?" And the King will answer them, "Truly, I say to you, as you did it to one of the least of these my brothers, you did it to me."
>
> Then he will say to those on his left, "Depart from me, you cursed, into the eternal fire prepared for the devil and his angels. For I was hungry and you gave me no food, I was thirsty and you gave me no drink, I was a stranger and you did not welcome me, naked and you did not clothe me, sick and in prison and you did not visit me." Then they also will answer, saying, "Lord, when did we see you hungry or thirsty or a stranger or naked or sick or in prison, and did not minister to you?" Then he will answer them, saying, "Truly, I say to you, as you did not do it to one of the least

of these, you did not do it to me." And these will go away into eternal punishment, but the righteous into eternal life.

How are Christians today treating the least of these? The immigrant? The refugee? The foreigner? The homeless? The hungry? The weak? The sick? The persecuted, oppressed, alienated, ignored, abused, and maligned? We can do a lot better. Followers of Christ should be especially attentive to anyone who is being exploited or afflicted. "Will we be seen as a people who sacrificially laid down their lives for the gospel, who served and stood with the poor, the oppressed and the marginalized?" asks pastor and author Jo Saxton. "Will we be seen as a people who stood complicit in the things that kept people bound and oppressed, self-serving and committed to our own privilege? Will we be seen as the people who were the problem, or those who fought, serve[d], [spoke] towards the solutions, even in our human frailty?"[16]

Hate and ignorance can fuel Christendom's tendency to hurt and abandon the least of these, but Christians' motives aren't always blatantly sinister. There are many rational reasons that prevent people from helping the least of these. These reasons might include security or economic, social, or political interests. But frankly, there are no theological ones. As Christians, we have committed to following Jesus, which means pursuing the most loving outcomes possible regardless of whether they're the most reasonable. A particular action or decision might not be the smartest stance according to your political party, the safest option according to your security analyst, or the most lucrative strategy according to your financial advisor. But no priority should ever trump the gospel. According to Jesus, no reason can outweigh the importance of helping the least of these.

One form of goodness should never need to undermine another. For example, Jesus isn't going to abandon refugees in order to save immigrants. He's not going to reject the homeless in order to protect the lives of unborn babies and children. He's not going to ignore the sick so that he can feed the hungry. Following Jesus isn't an either/or proposition, and any time you feel as if you're faced with a choice that involves deciding between the lesser of two evils, you're no longer engaging with Jesus. In those cases, you're being given falsehoods, because God doesn't sacrifice the least of *these* for least of *those*. The love of Jesus doesn't compromise, choose sides, or abandon and forget about anybody, and neither should we.

Jesus never deported an immigrant. Jesus never refused help to a refugee. Jesus never blamed the poor. Jesus never killed an enemy. Jesus never banned a foreigner. Jesus never made anyone feel less than worthy because of their gender, race, legal status, political affiliation, nationality, or social standing. He healed enemies, he embraced the stranger, he accepted the outsider, he empowered the weak, and he sacrificed himself on a cross for the sake of *all* humanity.

MANIPULATE THE BIBLE TO BENEFIT YOURSELF

The greatest tool Christians use to circumvent the path of Jesus is the Bible itself. There's no stronger way to absolve ourselves from following Christ than the very Word of God, right?

So when Jesus says crazy stuff like "Love your enemies, do good to those who hate you" (Luke 6:27), we can counter with Genesis 9:6, which states, "Whoever sheds the blood of man, by man shall his blood be shed, for God made man in his own image." (See, if they kill one of us we can kill them!) And when Christ continues his lunatic ramblings by saying

"Sell your possessions, and give to the needy. Provide yourselves with moneybags that do not grow old, with a treasure in the heavens that does not fail, where no thief approaches and no moth destroys" (Luke 12:33), we're quick to honor the virtues of "stewardship" and reference verses like 1 Timothy 5:8, which warns, "But if anyone does not provide for his relatives, and especially for members of his household, he has denied the faith and is worse than an unbeliever." (God said to be a good steward with my money, so I'm not going to waste it on the poor!)

The Bible is at the mercy of the motivations of its readers. We can wield the Word of God to do both good and evil. When the devil tempted Jesus, he used one strategy against Christ over and over again: wielding Scripture against him. It didn't work. But we still try to use Scripture for our own purposes.

In her book *A Year of Biblical Womanhood*, Rachel Held Evans describes this process this way:

> If you are looking for verses with which to support slavery, you will find them. If you are looking for verses with which to abolish slavery, you will find them. If you are looking for verses with which to oppress women, you will find them. If you are looking for verses with which to liberate or honor women, you will find them. If you are looking for reasons to wage war, you will find them. If you are looking for reasons to promote peace, you will find them. If you are looking for an outdated, irrelevant ancient text, you will find it. If you are looking for truth, believe me, you will find it.
>
> This is why there are times when the most instructive question to bring to the text is not *what does it say?* but *what am I looking for?* I suspect Jesus knew this when he said, "Ask and it will be given to you, seek and you will find, knock and the door will be opened." If you want to do violence in this world, you will always find the weapons. If you want to heal, you will always find the balm.[17]

Virtually any conviction or action can be either supported or criticized using the Bible. Rich Mullins once pointed out, "We do need to be born again, since Jesus said that to a guy named Nicodemus. But if you tell me I have to be born again to enter the kingdom of God, I can tell you that you have to sell everything you have and give it to the poor, because Jesus said that to one guy too. . . . But I guess that's why God invented highlighters, so we can highlight the parts we like and ignore the rest."[18]

When interpreting and implementing "biblical truth," well-meaning believers can arrive at completely opposite conclusions. Society also continually forces us to decipher new and complicated issues that the Bible may not address at all, and there are moral topics our ancient verses don't offer any definitive answers to. Despite all our prayers and seeking, we may never get a conclusive response that satisfies our desire for further clarity. This is just one reason that Christians need to show extraordinary amounts of grace and love to others. It's within these tensions, the vast grey areas of our spirituality, where we must rely on the peace of God, "which surpasses all understanding, [and] will guard your hearts and your minds in Christ Jesus" (Philippians 4:7).

SAY "JESUS IS IMPOSSIBLE TO FOLLOW!"

There are other methods for avoiding Christ. The fact that Jesus went through everything without ever sinning is a common excuse people give for not following his example. "Jesus was able to do all of that because he was the Son of God," we say. "He was divine and we are not, so we shouldn't be held to those same standards."

The very reason we worship and praise Jesus—his divinity, his identity as God incarnate—is given as a pretext to avoid emulating his actions. This reasoning not only downplays the humanity of Jesus; it also fails to recognize the power and ability we've been given through the Holy Spirit. Wanting to be like Jesus is easy to say but undeniably hard to do, but we should never view the life of Jesus as an unrealistic path to follow. Christ himself said, "If anyone would come after me, let him deny himself and take up his cross and follow me" (Matthew 16:24).

We must meditate deeply on what role the life of Jesus is meant to play in our lives. Jesus is the very essence of God and God's glory. "He is the image of the invisible God, the firstborn of all creation. For by him all things were created, in heaven and on earth, visible and invisible, whether thrones or dominions or rulers or authorities—all things were created through him and for him. And he is before all things, and in him all things hold together" (Colossians 1:15-17). "He is the radiance of the glory of God and the exact imprint of his nature, and he upholds the universe by the word of his power. After making purification for sins, he sat down at the right hand of the Majesty on high" (Hebrews 1:3). Are these passages only to remind us of how wonderful Jesus was and is, or are they also meant to provide us a blueprint for how to act?

Yes, Jesus loved us enough to die for our sins. But he also loved us enough to show us how to live.

EMBRACE LOVELESS THEOLOGY

Few Christians deny the importance of love, yet it can be found wanting within Christendom. "Christian" messages can be anything but loving, and Christianity is routinely sabotaged by public personalities who claim to be ambassadors of Christ while simultaneously being nothing like Christ.

Using the Bible for our own purposes is one tactic to avoid modeling the life of Christ; using theology to bypass love is another. If your theology—the study of God—isn't motivated by love, doesn't inspire you to love, and doesn't produce love, you're doing theology wrong. Love is the product of good theology, and anything besides love is the result of bad theology. Love-based theology is what empowers Christians to help others, know God better, and mature spiritually. But theology *without* love is responsible for some of the world's worst moments.

Loveless theology led to the Crusades, fueled the Inquisition, caused frenzied witch hunts, rationalized slavery, and excuses racism. Loveless theology promotes sexism, justifies wars, and explains away genocide. It embraces violence while reconciling hate. Without love, theology is utterly worthless —even if you wholeheartedly believe you have the "right" theology. Beyond the realm of churches, seminary classrooms, Christian blogs, and a few other religious platforms, nobody really cares about what you believe. But people will care about how you act, what you say, and how you say it.

When you bring a hot meal to a sick friend, your friend won't care what version of the Bible you read. The stranger to whom you return a lost wallet won't care if you're a Calvinist or an open theist. When you visit a lonely senior citizen, he won't care what church you attend. If you adopt an orphan, that child won't care who your favorite theologian is. When you give food to a person who is homeless, she won't care about your opinions regarding infant baptism. Love matters most.

Unfortunately, many Christians love theology more than they love people, and loveless theology has caused harm on a massive scale. Loveless theology fuels the worst parts of our sinful nature—pitting believer against believer, believer against nonbeliever, and believer against God. When used to alienate and devalue others, theology can be weaponized and turned into a spiritual form of aggression.

NO PERFECT FORMULA OTHER THAN LOVE

As we've seen, it's easy to avoid following Jesus. There are lots of ways to do so, and many of us have tried one or more of them at various points.

There's no perfect formula for following Christ, and reducing discipleship to a few easy steps is impossible. The single most important criteria of the Christian life is how well you accept and exude the nature of Jesus. If you're unsure about the nature of Jesus and how to follow him, the Bible goes out of its way to reiterate it over and over again—it's love. First John 4:16 tells us, "God is love, and whoever abides in love abides in God, and God abides in him." We're also told, "Anyone who does not love does not know God, because God is love" (1 John 4:8).

When asked, Jesus himself declared that the two greatest commandments are rooted in love: "And one of them, a lawyer, asked him a question to test him. 'Teacher, which is the great commandment in the Law?' And he said to him, 'You shall love the Lord your God with all your heart and with all your soul and with all your mind. This is the great and first commandment. And a second is like it: You shall love your neighbor as yourself. On these two commandments depend all the Law and the Prophets'" (Matthew 22:35-40).

And being rooted in love is at the center of what is often called "the love chapter": 1 Corinthians 13. In this chapter the apostle Paul writes:

Love is patient, love is kind. It does not envy, it does not boast, it is not proud. It does not dishonor others, it is not self-seeking, it is not easily angered, it keeps no record of wrongs. Love does not delight in evil but rejoices with the truth. It always protects, always trusts, always hopes, always perseveres.

Love never fails. But where there are prophecies, they will cease; where there are tongues, they will be stilled; where there is knowledge, it will pass away. For we know in part and we prophesy in part, but when completeness comes, what is in part disappears. When I was a child, I talked like a child, I thought like a child, I reasoned like a child. When I became a man, I put the ways of childhood behind me. For now we see only a reflection as in a mirror; then we shall see face to face. Now I know in part; then I shall know fully, even as I am fully known.

And now these three remain: faith, hope and love. But the greatest of these is love. (1 Corinthians 13:4-13 NIV)

To this day, one of the most memorable things a pastor has ever done for me was bring me a leftover Thanksgiving meal. I was at work, and it was near midnight. Earlier that evening our church had held a Thanksgiving meal that I couldn't attend. As a college student trying to eke out a living, I couldn't afford to take any time off work—and also had the least amount of seniority—so I was stuck working the Thanksgiving shift.

Knowing that I would still be working the late shift, my pastor and his wife took a cab across town and surprised me at my job to personally deliver the food themselves.

The entire exchange lasted less than two minutes. My pastor got out of the cab, handed me the Tupperware container full of food, said a few pleasantries, then climbed back in the cab to head home. I was completely overwhelmed by this small gesture of love.

Of all the thousands of hours my pastor spent preparing sermons and teaching all sorts of wonderful theology, the greatest way his entire ministry influenced me consisted of some leftover turkey and gravy.

7

Citizens of Another Country

But seek first the kingdom of God and his righteousness.
—MATTHEW 6:33

I pledge allegiance to the Flag of the United States of America, and to the Republic for which it stands, one Nation under God, indivisible, with liberty and justice for all."

If you live in the United States, like me, you've probably recited this numerous times, whether while in elementary school or at some sort of civic ceremony. But as a Christian, have you ever really reflected on the words you're saying?

When you say the pledge, you are pledging your life to something fallible, human-made, lifeless. You are pledging loyalty to a thing that's not God and doesn't even represent God. Patriotism should never obscure righteousness, and nationalism should never trump holiness. Our worship of Christ should never be compromised by our allegiance to any earthly ruler, country, or political manifesto. The United States of America isn't the kingdom of God. That's a truth we seem to have forgotten. It's not uncommon for churches to celebrate the Fourth of July, honor military personnel and veterans, adorn sanctuaries with flags, and incorporate America into songs of worship.

For the very first followers of Jesus, these nationalistic symbols and practices would have been alarming and even considered blasphemous. Jesus didn't preach next to a Roman standard or honor Roman soldiers for slaughtering enemies of the state. Early believers considered being pro-empire antithetical to being members of the kingdom of God. For the believers in the early church, being a good follower of Jesus sometimes meant being a horrible citizen of Rome. Could the same be true for us today?

All Christians are dual citizens, governed by both a worldly empire and a divine one. When the two conflict with each other, as they often do, which authority are Christians called to serve? The answer is clear, although it is not easy. The apostle Paul reminds us that "our citizenship is in heaven, and from it we await a Savior, the Lord Jesus Christ" (Philippians 3:20).

This chapter reckons with the concept of citizenship, which has tripped up so many Christians living within Christendom. We examine Scripture passages that have been used to justify ultimate allegiance to nation and service to the state. And we look at the words of Jesus, who calls us to pledge allegiance not to nation but to himself.

HUMANITY'S DESIRE FOR POLITICAL POWER

The Bible repeatedly warns us that political power is detrimental to one who aims to become holy and righteous. When Samuel became old, he named his sons judges over Israel. But his sons were corrupt, and as a result, the people began asking for a king.

Then all the elders of Israel gathered together and came to Samuel at Ramah and said to him, "Behold, you are old and your sons do not walk in your ways. Now appoint for us a king to judge us like all the nations." But the thing displeased Samuel when they said, "Give us a king to judge us." And Samuel prayed to the Lord. And the Lord said to Samuel, "Obey the voice of the people in all that they say to you, for they have not rejected you, but they have rejected me from being king over them. According to all the deeds that they have done, from the day I brought them up out of Egypt even to this day, forsaking me and serving other gods, so they are also doing to you. Now then, obey their voice; only you shall solemnly warn them and show them the ways of the king who shall reign over them."

So Samuel told all the words of the Lord to the people who were asking for a king from him. He said, "These will be the ways of the king who will reign over you: he will take your sons and appoint them to his chariots and to be his horsemen and to run before his chariots. And he will appoint for himself commanders of thousands and commanders of fifties, and some to plow his ground and to reap his harvest, and to make his implements of war and the equipment of his chariots. He will take your daughters to be perfumers and cooks and bakers. He will take the best of your fields and vineyards and olive orchards and give them to his servants. He will take the tenth of your grain and of your vineyards and give it to his officers and to his servants. He will take your male servants and female servants and the best of your young men and your donkeys, and put them to his work. He will take the tenth of your flocks, and you shall be his slaves. And in that day you will cry out because of your king, whom you have chosen for yourselves, but the Lord will not answer you in that day."

But the people refused to obey the voice of Samuel. And they said, "No! But there shall be a king over us, that we also may be like all the nations, and that our king may judge us and go out before us and fight our battles." (1 Samuel 8:4-20)

Despite almost every single king in the Old Testament being a failure and God's repeated frustration with his people asking for a political representative, people still somehow believe in the power of government rulers.

Every new election demonstrates just how obsessive U.S. politicians become in their efforts to woo Christian voters into embracing their policies. This desperation is matched by that of many Christians themselves, who see political power as an opportunity to advance their faith. Christians who are invested in Christendom leverage their support to broker certain outcomes. But sometimes legislating Christian morality comes at a much steeper price—sacrificing the kingdom of God for the kingdoms of mortals.

In Matthew 6:33, Jesus commands us to "seek first the kingdom of God," and in John 18:36 he explicitly says, "My kingdom is not of this world. If my kingdom were of this world, my servants would have been fighting, that I might not be delivered over to the Jews. But my kingdom is not from the world."

It's important to realize that the political parties of this earth aren't the kingdom of God, nor will they ever be. The Bible even suggests that instead of God being sovereign over them—which many Christians claim—Satan himself may control them. First John 5:19 states that "the whole world lies in the power of the evil one." The greatest thing Satan believed he could tempt Jesus with was political power:

The devil took him to a very high mountain and showed him all the kingdoms of the world and their glory. And he said to him, "All these I will give you, if you will fall down and worship me." Then Jesus said to him, "Be gone, Satan! For it is written, 'You shall worship the Lord your God and him only shall you serve'" (Matthew 4:8-10).

You shall worship the Lord your God and him only: these are important words to remember, especially for Christians struggling to balance political convictions with spiritual ones. Jesus reiterated the significance of knowing what we worship when he said, "No one can serve two masters, for either he will hate the one and love the other, or he will be devoted to the one and despise the other. You cannot serve God and money" (Matthew 6:24).

Now replace the word *money* with "the Republican Party" or "the Democratic Party" or "the United States of America." Politics and money are often essentially one and the same thing.

In any case, Christians should be sobered by how firmly Jesus made this point. If and when you ever have to choose between a politician, political party, government, and Jesus, always choose Christ. "We must obey God rather than any human authority" (Acts 5:29 NRSV).

RENDER TO CAESAR

Christians who live in a culture in which their faith remains socially and politically dominant might find it hard to accept that the dictates of their God and the demands of their country could ever contradict each other. Christians sometimes use Jesus' words as support for their nationalism, citing the time that Christ said, "Render to Caesar the things that are Caesar's, and to God the things that are God's" (Matthew 22:21).

The meaning of this text is stated right in the verse, yet many fail to see it. Jesus is clearly saying that the Roman emperor, Caesar, *is not God*. He is making a distinction between the Roman Empire and God. The empire and God are completely separate entities, not to be confused with one another. The government and God are so disconnected, in fact, that they require two completely different offerings. Instead of suggesting that Christians should respectfully submit to their ruling governments, Jesus is implying the opposite. He is subversively declaring that Caesar and his kingdom aren't in any way, shape, or form related to God. For that time and place, Jesus' words were a treasonous statement. This sentence, which is today so often used to justify nationalistic faith, could have resulted in Jesus' death.

In a way, of course, it did.

BE SUBJECT TO GOVERNING AUTHORITIES

Another verse that Christians regularly use to rationalize their political allegiances is Romans 13:1: "Let every person be subject to the governing authorities. For there is no authority except from God, and those that exist have been instituted by God."

Of all the verses that would seem to deny Satan's realm on earth, this is the strongest. Yet this verse must be read in the context of the larger passage in which it is located, which calls followers of Jesus to what theologian Ted Grimsrud calls "an all-encompassing, suffering love of their fellow believers (12:10) and their enemies (12:21) and everyone in between." Grimsrud and others also suggest that the word translated "authorities" in this passage is the Greek word for "powers," which elsewhere in Scripture refers not to particular governments but to the principalities and powers that govern behind the scenes.[1] We cannot ensure that the dictates of any particular government will *never* disagree with our greatest Christian responsibility: to love God and love others.

And what about Christians living in North Korea, Syria, China, Iran, Iraq, Afghanistan, Russia? Are we to read Romans 13:1 as ordering them to faithfully submit to their government and political leaders as well? Is the Bible commanding Christians throughout the world to submit to dictators, ruthless regimes, genocidal leaders, and authoritarian empires?

Following governmental laws and submitting to their authority should never compromise following God. If it does, then we're clearly told to follow God rather than our government. Loyalty to God and God's kingdom must always supersede our allegiance to nation. Paul reminds us in Ephesians that Jesus Christ is our peace. He writes, "You are citizens with the saints and also members of the household of God" (Ephesians 6:19). When our citizenship with the saints conflicts with our citizenship of this world, we must make a choice. We choose our identity in Christ instead of love for a nation. We choose Jesus instead of Caesar.

God should always be prioritized over any government. This is a simple truth, loaded with controversy. Many believers find this impossible to do, and it may be hard to comprehend how the two could ever be separated from one another in the first place. In America, many churches have embraced patriotism without really reflecting on the spiritual sacrifices they're making in the process. Christians who propose that the government and its laws should be the ultimate authority, and that we should be "law-abiding citizens" no matter what, often forget that some of the Bible's most esteemed figures were arrested and thrown in jail. Peter, John, Paul, Silas, and Stephen were all lawbreakers. Jesus himself was seized, put on trial, and crucified. All these actions were well within the laws of the Roman Empire. Most of the disciples and apostles faced martyrdom—often by the hands of government authorities— and members of the early church met a similar fate. These were the very first Christian resisters of government. The very origins of Christianity were in "lawlessness." From the perspective of the Roman Empire, Christians were criminals.

THE PARADOX OF POLITICS

Much of the failure of U.S. Christianity to address white supremacy, poverty, and violence is because of its unwillingness to betray political ideals. The ugly truth is that many white Christians have come to view the fight against racism as a liberal agenda. Providing benefits to the poor is seen as a Democrat-driven policy, and preventing violence through gun control is perceived as the ultimate betrayal of conservative ideals.

Conversely, the failure of liberal-leaning Christians to call former president Barack Obama to account for the increased number of drone strikes in Pakistan, Somalia, Yemen, and elsewhere during his presidency also reveals a political bias. Beyond increased militarization, Obama's administration also facilitated horrid family detention centers and immigration practices, and it failed to police systemic corporate and banking malpractices. Whether you're a Democrat, Republican, Libertarian, socialist, or anarchist, as a Christian, you should first and foremost do your best to live as Jesus did.

In one way, following Jesus *is* inherently political. When you try to emulate Christ by giving to the poor, caring for the sick, pursuing justice for the oppressed, and advocating for peace, you're inserting yourself into deeply political issues and conflicts. Yet the paradox is that the One in whom we put our hope and trust is not political, in the sense that his kingdom operates on an entirely different plane. This truth—we are political because we follow a nonpolitical Savior—is uncomfortable and messy. Christians must navigate through this by actively loving everyone and by remaining solely devoted to Christ.

Some Christians, in trying to get out of this bind, suggest that politics should be wholly separate from Christianity. But this claim is often made from a privileged position of comfort and power. It is made by people whose loved ones don't face the threat of deportation, who aren't the victims of systemic racism, who aren't being banned from entering a country, and who aren't being directly affected by the policies and actions of a government. While the kingdom of God won't arrive through the structures of government or politics, Christians can still use their right to vote, and their voices, to advocate for what they believe are the most Christlike policies.

In *The Myth of a Christian Nation*, theologian Gregory Boyd writes:

> Of course our political views will be influenced by our Christian faith. We may even believe that our views, if they are implemented, will help facilitate the advancement of the kingdom. But we must also recognize that people who have diametrically opposing views may believe *they too* are advancing the kingdom, which is all well and good as long as we don't christen our views as *the* Christian view. As people whose citizenship is in heaven before it is in any nation (Phil 3:20), and whose kingdom identity is rooted in Jesus rather than in any political agenda, we must never forget that

the only way we individually and collectively represent the kingdom of God is through loving, Christlike, sacrificial acts of service to others. Anything and everything else, however good and noble, lies outside the kingdom of God.[2]

When it comes to politics, Christianity is used as a bargaining chip and a way to gain votes. It's a cheap disguise, and Christians are routinely duped into believing they're participating in a holy movement rather than a political one.

Every era has shown the destructive consequences of marrying politics and faith. Looking at how Jesus navigated the paradoxes of politics is critical, and it may help Christians living within Christendom to parse out what it means to be faithful. "Consider these questions," writes Boyd:

> Did Jesus ever suggest by word of example that we should aspire to acquire, let alone take over, the power of Caesar? Did Jesus spend any time and energy trying to improve, let alone dominate, the reigning government of his day? Did he ever work to pass laws against the sinners he hung out with and ministered to? Did he worry at all about ensuring that his rights and the religious rights of his followers were protected? Does any author in the New Testament remotely hint that engaging in this sort of activity has anything to do with the kingdom of God? The answer to all these questions is, of course, no.[3]

RECKONING WITH THE LEGACY OF TRUMP

One cannot write about Christianity and politics after 2016 without writing about Donald Trump. White evangelical Christians are directly responsible for electing Donald Trump to the presidency of the United States. The harmful legacy of the 2016 election is one with which the church will have to reckon for years to come.

Many Christians and churches refuse to directly address the harmful policies and words of President Trump and his administration either for fear of causing conflict or simply because they want to remain in their positions of comfort and power. But to not talk about Trump is to ignore the biggest story currently facing Western Christianity.

Trump has publicly mocked people with disabilities, prisoners of war, and women. He has boasted about assaulting women and committing adultery. He has pushed xenophobic and racist rhetoric, and he has done and said so many disrespectful and horrifying things that it's hard to keep track of them all. All of this cannot be reconciled with verses like these: "But the fruit of the Spirit is love, joy, peace, patience, kindness, goodness, faithfulness, gentleness, self-control; against such things there is no law" (Galatians 5:22-23). "But the wisdom from above is first pure, then peaceable, gentle, open to reason, full of mercy and good fruits, impartial and sincere" (James 3:17). "Fools despise wisdom and instruction" (Proverbs 1:7).

Many white Christians have rationalized their support for Trump by saying things like "He was the best possible choice"; "Although I disagree with his actions, I support his policies"; and "He's a good example that God can use anybody to further his will!" Instead of holding Trump accountable for his many wrongdoings, many white evangelicals simply refuse to acknowledge his sinful behavior.

This partnership between Christians and Trump will have consequences for decades to come. Proverbs warns, "Leave the presence of a fool, for there you do not meet words of knowledge. The wisdom of the prudent is to discern his way, but the folly of fools is deceiving. Fools mock at the guilt offering, but the upright enjoy acceptance" (Proverbs 14:7-9), and it suggests that "whoever walks with the wise becomes wise, but the companion of fools will suffer harm" (Proverbs 13:20). The term *fool* may seem like a pretty tame description for somebody who could be called a lot worse. But in the Bible, *fool* is one of the most unfavorable labels imaginable. It's the very opposite of being wise and Christlike.

In many ways, Trump is simply the personification of years of Christian ideology that has united faith and politics. His election is the culmination of white evangelicals' tireless work and lobbying for political power for the sake of expanding a pseudo-Christian political state, in which Christians rule the government and enforce their own standards of morality through legislation and influence.

But the victory has come at a steep price. The authentic life of Christ has been completely masked by "Christian" activity in political campaigns and elections, and Christendom has traded in whatever remaining legitimacy it may have had for gaining congressional seats and capturing the White House. Sermons about the sanctity of marriage are now preached against the backdrop of support for a president who admitting to paying off a pornographic film actress to keep quiet about an alleged sexual encounter. Christian messages about valuing life now happen within the context of an expanding military budget, and the virtue of peace is now talked about within the context of leaders bragging about bombing our enemies. Homilies about honesty are now heard within the context of lying politicians. Virtues of love, joy, and peace sound especially empty coming from Christians who have supported misogynistic, racist, discriminatory, bigoted, xenophobic, and foolish leaders.

To an extent, we are all fools who lack wisdom. But the election of Donald Trump poses questions every white Christian in the United States must tackle. While the economy might flourish and some people may become wealthier, we will be forever challenged by the words of Christ, who asked, "What good is it for someone to gain the whole world, yet forfeit their soul?" (Mark 8:36 NIV).

When Christians publicly defend people of immoral character for the sake of "the greater good" or out of ignorance or spite, nonbelievers will rightfully shake their heads in disbelief and refuse to listen to anything we have to say. When Christians become known for their sullied politics, it makes witnessing and sharing the good news of Christ a whole lot harder.

Christian Witness in a Disillusioned Age

And he said to them, "Go into all the world and proclaim the gospel to the whole creation."
—MARK 16:15

I used to wear a WWJD (What Would Jesus Do?) bracelet in high school. It was my way of telling the world that I was a follower of Christ without actually having to talk about it. I assumed that people would see my bracelet, witness my angelic actions—or at least acknowledge I was a somewhat decent human being—and suddenly dedicate their lives to following Jesus. It didn't work.

So a few years later I tried again. This time I put a Christian fish decal on my car's bumper. Surely whoever drove past me during rush-hour traffic would see my divinely inspired patience and supernatural ability to avoid traffic accidents and credit my amazing driving and calm demeanor to a holy God. They would be so pleasantly surprised by my presence—standing out amid millions of other drivers—that they would visit their local church. It didn't work.

On to the third tactic: wearing a crucifix around my neck while playing sports. I got this idea from watching ESPN. Whenever I would score a goal while playing soccer or blow past someone with my lightning-bolt speed, people would be so impressed. Once they saw the cross I was wearing, they would be persuaded to convert to Christianity. Just in case they didn't see the cross, I thought, I would make sure to point to the sky or bring my hands to my chest to make a sign of the cross. Unfortunately, besides the fact that I could never score any goals, it didn't work.

Since associating myself with Christian things wasn't working, I started *disassociating* myself from things that weren't Christian. By noticing the things I didn't do, people would see that I was different from the world around me. And being so impressed with my counterculture lifestyle, they'd wonder what made me different. Eventually they'd discover that I loved and followed Jesus (this would have to happen through a supernatural revelation, of course, since I wasn't going to actually talk to them about God). So I lived a morally pure life. I didn't swear, I didn't drink alcohol, I didn't gamble, I didn't smoke, I didn't gossip, I didn't cheat, I didn't steal, I didn't watch R-rated movies (except for Mel Gibson's *The Passion of the Christ*), I didn't watch late-night cable, I didn't listen to secular radio stations, I didn't make rude jokes, and I didn't play violent video games. It didn't work either.

Eventually I wised up and modernized my evangelistic methods. I started posting Bible verses online, and I used my

Facebook and Twitter accounts to share profound Scripture verses. I reposted inspirational memes and viral stories of God's latest miracles. Now, finally, people would surely see these verses and be mesmerized by their truth, convicted by the Holy Spirit, and inspired to follow God. It didn't work.

Frustrated, I decided to educate myself on what I was doing wrong. I enrolled in a biblical seminary, where I obsessively read the Bible, pored over theology books, completed academic papers, studied church history, memorized ministry techniques, and listened to the world's top Christian leaders via conferences, videos, and podcasts—all in order to better evangelize the world around me. It didn't work.

Finally, desperate and simply out of ideas, I prayed, meditated on Scripture, worshiped with all my heart, soul, and mind, and did my best to emulate Jesus. Occasionally during these times I would sense the Holy Spirit urging me to share the good news of God's grace to specific people around me. But such notions seemed too illogical and crazy to act on, so I didn't even try. I assumed it wouldn't work.

TALK ABOUT JESUS—REALLY?

People want something genuine—not experiences that are manipulative or manufactured. They don't want to know about God; they want to know God. But sometimes even knowing God isn't good enough. Throughout the Bible, numerous individuals and entire communities met God, talked to God, and knew God, but still rebelled and rejected God. We believe in—and have relationships with, and acknowledge the existence of—our classmates and coworkers, but that doesn't guarantee that we'll have good relationships with them. Believing that God is real and acknowledging God's existence doesn't automatically translate to loving God. Remember, even Satan believes in God.

Convincing people that God exists—that God is a real, active, and living divine being—is a vital first step toward introducing people to Jesus. Frankly, neither is an easy job. Especially today.

There was only a brief time before the peaceful spread of the gospel by the early church degenerated into forms of martial conquest. For many centuries after Constantine, the primary tactic used to spread Christendom was through military force. The Crusades brought "Christianity" to the Muslim world; the Inquisition brought "Christianity" to the Spanish world; and eventually people brought "Christianity" to the "New World." Through widespread genocide, enslavement, and endless forms of subjugation and destruction, "Christianity" became the state-sponsored religion throughout much of the world.

Although violent takeovers are no longer perceived as acceptable forms of evangelism, Western Christians are still guilty of using political power, legislative processes, and even military action to "defend our Christian values." Forcing Christian agendas on others is still a present-day problem. Despite modern advances, the temptation to rule over others has passed from generation to generation, and even if we don't support the use of martial force, we can still be guilty of using excessive emotional and spiritual abuse in an effort to "convert" others. As we've seen throughout this book, the legacy of Christianity's failures is manifold and expansive. Sharing the good news of Jesus with people who have been hurt by Christianity has always been a tough slog. These days, when people associate Christ with the politicized and xenophobic church that bears his name, it's even harder.

Compounding the problem is one of the biggest pitfalls facing modern Christianity today: Christians don't want to evangelize. Western Christians have stopped sharing their faith with others on a personal level. Sharing your faith has become a social faux pas, a practice that's been abused and is now deeply stigmatized. Associated with images of shouting tel-evangelists, angry protesters waving hateful placards, pressure tactics, and unhealthy relational interactions, evangelism has become almost a bad word—not only among non-Christians but among Christians as well.

Even the most well-intentioned mission agencies can be destructive, and our immature attempts to "save the world" often cause more harm than good. Memoirs from Jamie Wright (*The Very Worst Missionary: A Memoir or Whatever*), Amy Peterson (*Dangerous Territory: My Misguided Quest to Save the World*), and D. L. Mayfield (*Assimilate or Go Home: Notes from a Failed Missionary on Rediscovering Faith*) delve into the very real possibility that Christian missions can be a disastrous arm of Christendom rather than a manifestation of Christ. Their voices serve as a vital form of accountability for a mission industry that can easily lose its way.

Yet despite all the baggage associated with evangelism, Christians are still called to share the good news of Jesus. We are instructed by Jesus to go and "make disciples of all nations, baptizing them in the name of the Father and of the Son and of the Holy Spirit, teaching them to observe all that I have commanded you" (Matthew 28:19-20).

Indeed, the only people more uncomfortable than unbelievers with proselytizing and evangelism are Christians themselves. When someone starts blatantly talking about Jesus, even those of us who are Christians may feel awkward and anxious.

But at some point, don't followers of Jesus Christ have to talk about him?

OUR OWN STRUGGLE TO BELIEVE

One of the obstacles to sharing our faith may be that we sometimes doubt it ourselves. Few Christians would admit this, but deep down, many of us struggle with doubt. We wonder, Where is God? Christians live within a larger culture that doesn't readily recognize the existence of miracles, demons, angels, heaven, hell, or even God. Years of living within a culture ambivalent toward supernatural spirituality can cause even the strongest Christians to question the reality of God.

Christians who live in technologically dependent societies are heavily influenced by consumerism, addicted to digital forms of entertainment, and driven by capitalism-induced desires. We crave efficiency, and we are accustomed to streamlined processes and expect the best and most advanced products on the market. Success is measured by quantitative data. Something must be proven and presented in a convincing way in order for us to accept it as true.

But Christianity requires faith, not certitude. The aspects of our faith are hardly provable. To some, Christian faith might even be seen as a type of psychological disorder, or at least spiritual gibberish from people who have lost touch with reality and are not to be taken seriously. It has become socially unacceptable for believers to say things like "I think God is telling me" or "The Holy Spirit really convicted me" or "God did something amazing the other day." In a world organized by Enlightenment rationality, these statements are too spiritual for many of us.

Can we believe in—and talk about—something so unbelievable? Christianity isn't a palpable object that can be measured, analyzed, or proven. Our faith often manifests itself in the spiritual realm, a place that "enlightened people" across the globe increasingly shy away from.

So we stop talking about God altogether. It usually happens slowly, over time. We start to downplay the reality of our relationship with God, even to ourselves. We begin to abandon any sense of personal relationship with God, and we may end up hiding our faith or abandoning our belief in God altogether.

The Bible is filled with stories that don't seem plausible by today's standards, and many seem fictional. Moses parting the sea. Donkeys talking. A man living in the belly of a whale. People walking on water. Water turning into wine. A man being raised from the dead. Even if we believe that some parts of Scripture are meant to be interpreted as metaphors and are not be taken literally, there remain hundreds of unexplainable miracles, events, and actions that can only be attributed to the divine and supernatural power of God. But this same God we read about in the Bible may seem absent from our present- day reality.

Of all the things Christians must face, I think this struggle with doubt requires the most bravery. There are no easy answers. We don't have to solve our own doubt before we share the good news of Jesus with others. But unfortunately, sometimes we do let our own doubts stop us from talking with others about God.

CHRISTIANITY'S TILT AWAY FROM SPIRITUALITY

In the hopes of making our faith palatable and rationale enough to appeal to nonbelievers, many Christians have embraced a kind of secular *non*-spirituality. In fact, some Christians are the most skeptical of all people when it comes to miracles, prophecies, signs, wonders, and any other form of unquantifiable divine revelation. If we *do* manage to talk to others about our faith, we may downplay the "crazy stuff" and drain it of its supernatural power.

Perhaps as insiders to the faith, we've been burned too many times. We've seen firsthand the damage of hucksters, shady religious schemes, corrupt church leaders, hypocritical churches, and a long list of spiritual cons and abusive practices. So when something unexplainable happens, we do our best to rationally explain it in the best way we know how: through our lifelong experience of living within a world that doesn't readily recognize God.

As Christians, we're almost afraid to admit the supernatural; we become embarrassed by referring to its existence. If someone is healed, we explain it medically. If someone overcomes an addiction, we assume their recovery was because of their willpower, a good rehab program, or familial support, instead of the power of God. Those who do glorify God in these instances are seen as religious fundamentalists who have an unhealthy perception of what is real and what is fake.

And while some Christians can overspiritualize everything, many of us have swung dangerously in the opposite direction. We now avoid and reject *anything* that appears to be supernatural, stigmatizing it as being sensationalistic and emotionally manipulative.

While it's true that many evangelists, street preachers, and traveling revivalists misuse the name of Christ, do you want to know a less popular and more sinister reason why Christians are wary of them? It's because, in many ways, these folks are acting more like Bible characters than the rest of us. Yes, sometimes our wariness is well placed. Such evangelists do have a history of committing crimes and bilking people out of money. But I sometimes wonder whether our skepticism is also a byproduct of being integrated into a society no longer comfortable with the spirit world.

In this way we've adopted a dangerously insular and ethnocentric faith, rejecting the very real spirituality of countless cultures by defaulting to a Western view of reality. We may still believe in God, but we're not willing to go much further. We're willing to accept a divine being as our Savior but unwilling to say that supernatural evil (Satan) or other entities (angels and demons) actually exist.

Angels, demons, powers we cannot see: they're too unbelievable, right? Churches in the United States and Canada today often fall into the mold that our culture prefers: modern, sleek, efficient, scientific, logical, consumer-centric, and business-oriented. Instead of spending time talking to God, we spend our time talking about God. Elder boards are filled with corporate executives. Pastors manage churches like CEOs, planning expansion projects that emulate Fortune 500 companies rather than any Christ-centered vision. Ministries are outsourced. Media is updated. Content is streamlined. Time is efficiently scheduled, and services are produced and rehearsed. Worship is a show, and mission trips are marketed as quasi vacations. Instead of being countercultural, Christians are accommodating.

Yes, we must adapt and present the message of Jesus in a culturally relevant way. This is how much of today's Christian culture operates: adopt customs and adapt the gospel. A major Christian strategy of evangelism has been to look identical to the world around us. The motivations behind this are to be less judgmental, more approachable, and increasingly open and hospitable to the surrounding community—all very good things. But sometimes we are so accommodating that there's no noticeable difference between Christianity and the society to which it is attempting to minister. Sometimes we sacrifice our spirituality—our personal relationship and connection with God—on the altar of relevance.

It's not just megachurches appealing to seekers that are guilty of extreme accommodation; mainline churches fall into similar pitfalls. Even the most liturgical Christian traditions today are only shadows of their original selves. Years of subtle cultural adaptations and slow changes have taken something that was at one point in history considered to be extremely radical and progressive and transformed it into what is conventional. Martin Luther was considered a revolutionary, yet many of the churches that bear his name are the most resistant to change. All forms of Christianity adapt the faith to some degree. The message of Jesus becomes so wrapped in secular trappings that it is almost unrecognizable.

THE RISE OF "LIFESTYLE EVANGELISM"

Many Christians have bought into an evangelism strategy of subtle avoidance. The basic premise of what has been called "lifestyle evangelism" is that our moral and loving actions will speak louder than our words. The concept revolves around the assumption that people will see the radically different lifestyles of Christians and ultimately be moved to accept Jesus Christ as their Lord and Savior. But in reality, Christians haven't cornered the market on morality or kindness or love.

The stadium. The mall. The grocery store. The street traffic. The workplace. The school. Publicly gauging the spiritual health of others is not as easy as Christians sometimes think. You simply can't always tell who is or isn't a follower of Christ on the basis of a person's actions or relationships. Many Christians aren't very nice and are guilty of doing horrible things. Many non-Christians are the most generous and loving people around.

The entire practice of lifestyle evangelism also focuses on a "we're happier, we're better, and we're more holy than you" premise—not exactly a great selling point, especially when it's not even true. Yes, we who follow Jesus do try to glorify Christ through our daily actions. But for the most part, beyond official religious ceremonies and practices, there's often no noticeable difference between Christians and non-Christians. This lack of distinction is damning to a faith outspoken about its uniqueness.

OUTSOURCING EVANGELISM

Christians have found one particularly ingenious way to circumvent evangelism: outsourcing. Whether out of apathy or to avoid facing the harsh realities of evangelism—being vulnerable, sharing our testimony, risking relationships, or feeling awkward about talking about deep and spiritual things—we pass on the responsibility of fulfilling Christ's mandate to reach out to others. We strike a consumer-centric approach to evangelism, in which the sharing of faith is facilitated through corporate-like enterprises: events, concerts, communication campaigns, and special promotions. This way, the task of evangelism is no longer the responsibility of the individual but of a specialized "ministry team," nonprofit organization, or even business.

So prevalent is this strategy that many Christians have abandoned the idea that individuals should share their faith with words. In the same way we pay money to a cable company for wireless service, or a waste-management corporation to pick up our trash, or a landscape business to mow our lawns, we now pay others to "do ministry." We pay people to do spiritual work for us.

As Christians, we are often less comfortable introducing people to God than we are introducing them to everything *but* God: our preferred denomination, church, podcast, and theologian. We promote our brand of Christianity and are on the lookout for new customers rather than new Christ-followers. Evangelism should never become a method of shilling for anything or anyone other than God.

Christians should know better than anyone that there's no perfect formula for knowing God. You may have opinions about what churches are better and which theologians are more "biblical." But as with Christendom itself, churches and individuals are all imperfect representations of a perfect God. Any form of evangelism that's meant to promote anything other than God is merely an idolized form of selling, and it will leave people dissatisfied with a product that can never replace what can only be fulfilled by a divine love.

WE AREN'T THE FINAL BURDEN OF PROOF

At some point, Christians actually have to intentionally and clearly communicate Jesus to others. We don't do this because we want people to experience a lifestyle change or gain wealth or because the Bible tells us to. We witness to the life-changing power of Jesus because we want people to have a real, personal, and loving relationship with him. So as it relates to helping others believe in God, does the burden of proof lie with us? Yes and no.

Jesus told his disciples, "The harvest is plentiful, but the laborers are few; therefore pray earnestly to the Lord of the harvest to send out laborers into his harvest" (Matthew 9:37-38). That we're commanded to tell others about God is a point commonly accepted among Christians. We know this, and we've heard it a million times throughout our lifetime: Go preach the good news of Jesus to the world!

But the burden doesn't entirely rest on our shoulders. God is at work in the lives of others, and we can trust that truth. Many Christians have a hard time accepting that God is a living, breathing, active personality. But the reality is that right here, right now, in this exact moment and in every moment that is to come, an all-present, all-powerful, and all-knowing God is working toward a relationship with humanity. Hebrews 13:8 promises us that "Jesus Christ is the same yesterday and today and forever." This God doesn't want a passive, on-again, off-again relationship, but a deep, all-consuming relationship greater than any you've ever known or experienced or imagined. "For God so loved the world, that he gave his only Son, that whoever believes in him should not perish but have eternal life" (John 3:16).

This is a radical idea that's hard for many—even Christians—to accept. God loves people! So when you witness to others, be comforted and inspired by the fact that God is passionately and actively working at your side—divinely laboring with you, despite you, and beyond you. As you evangelize, the Spirit of God will be working with you and through you. "But you will receive power when the Holy Spirit has come upon you, and you will be my witnesses in Jerusalem and in all Judea and Samaria, and to the end of the earth" (Acts 1:8).

Others will come to know and experience a loving God not through our ability but through God's grace. This is where our trust should ultimately lie when we express our faith. God not only wants to do something good; God wants to do something good through us.

TRUSTING GOD'S LOVE FOR YOU AND THE WORLD

In order to believe that God wants to have a relationship with others, you must first truly believe that God wants that type of relationship with you. Do you have that type of relationship with God? Not with Christian culture, but with God? Romans 8:38-39 has it right when it says, "For I am sure that neither death nor life, nor angels nor rulers, nor things present nor things to come, nor powers, nor height nor depth, nor anything else in all creation, will be able to separate us from the love of God in Christ Jesus our Lord." Accepting that God desperately loves you and everyone around you changes everything. Believing that the Holy Spirit will move in people's lives is a first step.

Pray for people to discover that God loves them, and pray that they might know God. Evangelism hinges on the belief that God will facilitate an active relationship founded on love. Be bold enough to risk your reputation on the truth that God is real. It's this last point that we must ultimately believe in order to confidently share the good news with others: God is the final burden of proof.

Just as we invite others to conversion—to turn toward Christ and the love that he offers—so too we as believers must be open to change. Conversion is not only for people who do not yet know Jesus; we who have been trying to follow him for a long time must be always on the lookout for the ways Jesus wants to transform us.

9

The Christian Virtue of Change

Therefore, if anyone is in Christ, he is a new creation. The old has passed away; behold, the new has come.
—2 CORINTHIANS 5:17

I'm not proud of certain moments in my past. God, forgive me for my sinful, hurtful words and actions. I have said things like "Stop being so gay!" and "Quit acting like a retard!" I bullied classmates in college and stole people's food from dorm refrigerators. I used to think all poor people were lazy, all people of color were unjustly angry toward white people, and all Democrats were minions of Satan. I thought it was sinful for women to become pastors and that it was evil to consume alcohol, and I believed the United States of America could do no wrong.

Looking back, I wonder how I could have possibly believed and done and said things that are so completely opposite of who I understand Christ to be. I'm sad about the things I've done and said, and I've asked for forgiveness from God and others. Thank God that it's never too late to change.

Why are some Christians so adamantly opposed to change? Within Christendom, people often associate change with the worst possible scenarios. For example, if someone at your church hears that you have "changed" your beliefs about marriage, or the Bible, or Jesus—without being given any specific details—that person may automatically assume that your change has been a negative one.

It's also our natural tendency to believe that *we*—not *they*—know best. Thus if you change in a way that makes you different from the "us" of your church, others may instinctively think you have made a mistake. No matter what we believe about God, we believe we're right. Other people—who believe differently than we do—are the ones who aren't reading the right version of the Bible. They are the ones who misinterpret the end-times prophecies. They are the ones "doing church" wrong.

People who change may find themselves rejected by their Christian community. Or they may voluntarily leave, assuming—often rightfully so—that Christendom is too inflexible to accommodate them. Christian culture simply doesn't lend itself to change, and change isn't easy within religious environments that value uniformity from birth until death. Institutionalized Christianity expects you to learn, keep, and maintain the same theological doctrines for life. You are invited to accept a belief system that is permanent, unchanging, and not open to revision. The irony is that while there are countless traditions and communities within Christendom, each has constructed an atmosphere of spiritual permanence. Theoretically, a follower of Christ could participate in religious activities throughout childhood and adulthood—including Sunday school and youth group—within a church, denomination, and spiritual community and never undergo any spiritual changes. What should change and what should stay the same?

The more we grow in our faith, the more we realize we don't have it all figured out. Christianity becomes more complex with time. This doesn't make it any less fulfilling or meaningful. But many Christians refuse to embrace this complexity because it requires them to admit that they cannot always access truth. That can be a scary proposition. Should we be willing to change all our understandings and beliefs, or just some of them? Which ones should we hold on to with passion and depth, and which ones can we hold more lightly?

Gregory Boyd offers a helpful way to view our theology and beliefs as we consider the topic of change.

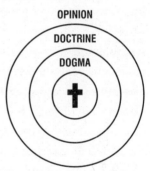

Think of your Christian beliefs as a set of concentric circles, with Jesus standing in the very center. In this illustration, Christ is represented by the cross. Jesus is the core; as the apostle Paul writes, "In him all things hold together" (Colossians 1:17).

From Gregory A. Boyd, "How to Talk about Theology," ReKnew, June 2, 2015, www.reknew.org/2014/06/how-to-talk-about-theology/. Used with permission.

From there, we move outward from dogma to doctrine to opinion. Boyd helpfully defines dogma, represented by the circle closest to the cross, as "our foundational ecumenical creeds (e.g., the Nicene and the Apostles' Creed). The belief that God is a Trinity, that Christ is fully God and fully human, and that the world is created and governed by God are examples of the dogmas that compose the innermost ring."[1]

From dogma we move to doctrine. Boyd defines the doctrine as "beliefs that orthodox Christians have always espoused, but over which there has been some disagreement. These are the different doctrines that distinguish various denominations, and most derive from different ways of interpreting the dogmas found in the ring just outside the core circle." For example, churches may practice different variations of baptism and communion, applying their unique theological interpretations to how the sacraments are practiced.

Finally, the realm of opinion is the furthest one from the cross. Boyd describes opinion, which occupies the final ring, as "beliefs that individual Christians have occasionally espoused but that have never gained widespread support and that have rarely been adopted by a recognized church body." Boyd gives two examples of opinions, which are ways of interpreting doctrines: the "gap theory," which suggests a way that the Genesis account of creation can be reconciled with evolution, and the "open view of the future," which maintains that "the future is not fully settled."[2] Gender roles within church leadership and the different interpretations of heaven and hell are examples of theological opinions.

So much of what disrupts people's faith has nothing to do with the centrality of Jesus. When people begin changing their theological beliefs, people in the church sometimes assume that they are no longer committed to Christ. In reality, many Christians change their opinions and their understanding of doctrines without weakening their commitment to Jesus or the central dogmas of the faith.

We must allow grace and mercy to guide us as we encounter believers who don't share our spiritual DNA. For example, I appreciate many theologians, pastors, and Christian leaders even if I don't completely agree with everything they preach. Some Christians will always find it hard to acknowledge that any truth or wisdom exists beyond their own beliefs, and they will distrust anyone or anything that may contradict their own worldview. To some extent we're all guilty of this. Most of us even disagree with the Christians whose beliefs and opinions most resemble our own. I disagree with my wife about some things and my pastor about others. Sometimes I even disagree with *myself*! But just because we may find a flaw in others—or ourselves—doesn't mean we should reject them. We may disagree with their opinions or doctrines, but we remain committed to the same Jesus. We must always remember, "Judgment is without mercy to one who has shown no mercy. Mercy triumphs over judgment" (James 2:13).

Eventually, if begrudgingly, I must admit that even Christians who represent traditions, theologies, or ideas I'm opposed to carry wisdom and truth from which I can learn. Sometimes I'm the one who is misguided, misinformed, or simply flat-out wrong.

Nobody has a corner on the market of truth, knowledge, wisdom, or God. Recognizing complexity doesn't negate believing in truth, and a diversity of opinion doesn't weaken the gospel. Jesus remains at the center.

CHRISTIANITY REQUIRES CHANGE

In the New Testament, Paul compares our faith to a marathon: a long, grueling, arduous race. Once you become a Christian, you don't automatically reach the pinnacle or magically teleport to the finish line of your spiritual race. As a new believer, you don't receive a divine revelation of everything there is to know about God. Doctrines don't suddenly become crystal clear, transcendent knowledge isn't immediately uploaded into your brain, and the perfect theology isn't miraculously inherited. You don't have it all figured out, and you never will.

Our faith is a path filled with ups and downs and changes. We slowly move from point A toward point Z, sometimes—maybe often—regressing in the process. Our faith won't be perfected by the time we're done with Sunday school, or after we've listened to a certain number of sermons, or graduated from seminary, or officially become a member of a particular church, or joined a certain denomination, or reached a certain age. Instead, we'll learn new things, live through different experiences, meet new people, and change our beliefs—and our faith in God—accordingly.

The influences that shape our beliefs are endless. A broken relationship may change the way we think about forgiveness. An abusive marriage may change the way we view divorce. The death of a child may change the way we talk about God's sovereignty, and falling in love may change the way we view marriage. A lifetime of relationships, experiences, and ideas will form the substance of our ever-evolving faith.

If you truly believe that God is all-knowing, all-present, and all-powerful, the sheer breadth and depth of God will always demand that we leave room for spiritual growth. "For my thoughts are not your thoughts, neither are your ways my ways, declares the Lord. For as the heavens are higher than the earth, so are my ways higher than your ways and my thoughts than your thoughts" writes Isaiah (Isaiah 55:8-9). The mystery of God is unending, always offering us something to learn and always leaving us room to change. In Romans, the apostle Paul reflects, "For who has known the mind of the Lord, or who has been his counselor?" (Romans 11:34).

I hope you don't have the exact same beliefs about God that you had when you were a child, a teenager, or even a year ago. Life causes your relationship with God, and your knowledge of God, to expand, grow, and mature.

In Scripture, the people who most hated change and who fought it the hardest were the Pharisees. Jesus frequently called the Pharisees to task for their inflexibility and unwillingness to consider new ways of seeing things. The problem with the Pharisees is that they *refused* to change, preferring their conventional piety and old traditions. They didn't want to think beyond their preconceptions or challenge their own assumptions, and they refused to question the beliefs to which they had devoted their lives.

The Pharisees are easy scapegoats, but it's important to realize that the disciples of Jesus—the ones who witnessed him perform miracles and healings, who heard firsthand his proclamations of divinity, and who spent so much time in his presence—were also slow to change. In fact, some of them were so uncertain about their faith that they abandoned Christ at the time of his death. It was only after his resurrection— after being personally visited by the risen Jesus himself—that they changed and were bold enough to go and proclaim the gospel. And even then they disagreed and debated about how to do so! If the very disciples of Jesus didn't have it all figured out, maybe we, too, can accept our uncertainty.

"I will give you a new heart and a new spirit I will put within you," Ezekiel writes. "I will remove the heart of stone from your flesh and give you a heart of flesh" (Ezekiel 36:26). This is just one of many verses demonstrating Scripture's focus on transformation as a central and recurring theme. In Scripture, people's encounters with God change them. The Israelites get back on track, the blind see, the sick are healed, the lame walk, and people are transformed—physically, emotionally, and spiritually. The people of God change from an old covenant to a new one, from legalism to grace, from their old selves to new selves. Drop everything you're doing and follow me! says Jesus. Become a new creation! We should wholeheartedly accept that "if anyone is in Christ, he is a new creation. The old has passed away; behold, the new has come" (2 Corinthians 5:17).

CHRISTENDOM REJECTS CHANGES

In an era of rapid social and technological change, it's not rare for people to change spiritual or theological beliefs quickly. Listening to a pastor or theologian on a podcast, reading a new book, talking with someone from a radically different faith background: such experiences make us ripe for changing our opinion about a particular topic. But while individuals have the capacity to make relatively quick and seamless changes in theology or worldview, institutions can't.

"Most people in America, when they are exposed to the Christian faith, are not being transformed," David Kinnaman and Gabe Lyons suggest. "They take one step into the door, and the journey ends. They are not being allowed, encouraged, or equipped to love or to think like Christ. Yet in many ways a focus on spiritual formation fits what a new generation is really seeking. Transformation is a process, a journey, not a one-time decision."[3]

Indeed, Christian institutions can be averse to change. Immediate change is impossible because the process involves official meetings, legislation, documentation, and votes to implement even the slightest alterations. Seminaries, denominations, and many congregations are full of bureaucracy and bylaws such that any change, however minor, becomes difficult. When someone disagrees with the status quo or agitates for change, authorities may enact disciplinary measures or people may simply leave rather than endure the thorny process required to ponder different opinions and consider implementing change. Thus, denominational and church splits are more common than institutional shifts. Changes do occur within Christendom, but usually they take years to occur or are instigated by a drastic event, disaster, or calamity.

This brings us to the next point: uniformity is self-serving. Much like businesses and corporations, institutions and communities within Christendom survive by promoting a particular brand or platform. They are attracting a theological clique, publicizing a distinctive vision, teaching a particular type of belief, and pursuing their own defined goals. Anything beyond their own beliefs, doctrines, and practices can be viewed as a threat or seen as "competition." New converts are immediately indoctrinated into a particular way of being Christian—not always for spiritual reasons but because one of the best ways to absorb people into a community is to preach conformity.

Frankly, it's easier for church leaders when everyone has the same beliefs. Sermons are easier to construct when you know what everyone believes theologically. Worship is easier to facilitate when you know which style everyone prefers.

Empowering others to embrace a different type of Christianity is rare. If someone in a faith community begins to change how they understand what it means to follow Jesus, it means the potential loss of a financial contributor and volunteer.

Institutions sometimes move into a defensive mode rather than find ways to support a parishioner's change. Churches sometimes even spiritually manipulate individuals into staying. It's rare to hear of pastors blessing members of the congregation on their way or lovingly directing a parishioner into a different community.

Those who work professionally in Christian ministry and church environments understand the rarity of this type of counsel. Many Christian leaders receive a salary, health insurance, retirement fund, and other benefits from their institution. What do they do when fulfilling their professional responsibilities runs against nurturing the spiritual interests of a particular member? Ideally, pastors and Christian leaders would affirm change as a main ingredient required for spiritual growth.

CHURCHES AND CHANGE

It has become common to bemoan "church shopping." The criticism is leveled against Christians who repeatedly hop from one faith community to the next, never willing to stick it out at one church for the long haul. This critique of a consumer model of church attendance has merit.

But in many ways the opposite has occurred. That is, churches have actually become so consumer-centric that they're unwilling to let people go. Christians are so insular and segmented that they refuse to trust in the larger and all-encompassing worldwide family of believers that exists beyond their own walls. They believe in *a* church more than they trust *the* church. So instead of freeing people and entrusting them to a different Christian community, they cling to their adherents, desperate to hold on to their own.

We all know of people who matured spiritually by changing—whether it was changing their church, their friends, or their beliefs. Sometimes change saves us and our faith. And we all know people who would be better off making some necessary changes.

Here's a message that Christian pastors, leaders, and laypeople must learn to accept: sometimes it's okay to go and to let others go. No church or community is perfect. In certain situations, for the sake of your faith and well-being, you must leave a particular congregation and find another one. Of course, don't depart for superficial reasons. Don't leave because your feelings got hurt, or because you don't like the way things are being done, or because it's just not your "style." Rather, you should leave if *not* leaving would destroy either your or your family's faith. Leave if you're suffering from spiritual, emotional, or physical abuse. Leave if your community is actually hurting instead of helping your faith in Christ. Do it because you're being called by God to leave, and because you have prayed and discerned that this is the most Christlike thing to do. In everything, follow Christ's example.

There will be times when we must stick it out and be disciplined, when courage is required and patience is needed to get through and resolve tough circumstances in a particular church community. But there is also a time, for some, when it becomes clear that changing church communities is the best option. God sometimes calls us to endure, but God also calls us to transform.

So while you may be called by God to leave a particular church institution, you will never be called by God to leave the church as a whole: the worldwide body of Christ that offers life-giving community, discipleship, worship, communion, and service. God insists that you experience deep fellowship and relational communion with other believers, but whether that happens within one particular church or another is beside the point. If others decide to depart your community of faith, try to empower, uplift, and be gracious. Don't kick them on the way out or discourage them. Help them find a new fellowship in which they can be nurtured in the way of Christ.

If people aren't given the option to change, instead of adjusting when they reach their spiritual breaking point, they may make a clean break and completely reject Christianity. We must selflessly point others to God, even if doing so means letting people depart from our fellowship or sending them off with a blessing into a new understanding of faith. This may feel like we're "losing" them. But if others are struggling with their relationship with Jesus or if they are in danger of abandoning Christ altogether, is it really wise to tell them to just keep plugging away? Is it beneficial for them to keep doing the same old thing?

CHRISTIAN LEADERS AND CHANGE

A hallmark of evangelical Christianity in the United States and Canada is the celebrity leader. Every megachurch, college, seminary, and nonprofit—even every theological perspective— usually has one or two well-known people who represent the group or institution. These individuals often associate a large part of their identity with their particular beliefs, and they have the most motivation—related to money, fame, recognition, power, influence, authority—to *not* change, because doing so would hurt their brand. Many of these people have developed their beliefs about God through years of experience and academic schooling, so they have a lot of knowledge to give credence to their teachings and beliefs. Ironically, the spiritual leaders who are the most *unchanging* are often the same ones who work the hardest to change the beliefs of others.

But as we've seen, latching on to a single belief or message or way of viewing God is not always conducive to faith development. When celebrity leaders make a single message a major part of their platform, what happens if or when they feel God leading them to change their minds or transform their perspectives? And if static spirituality and theological stagnation are not the way of Christ, why does Christendom promote this false hope—of unchanging perspectives—as the ideal for its leaders?

Unfortunately, we rarely see pastors or theologians confess that they have been wrong or admit that they have changed their minds. To do so would invite condemnation and ridicule, and it may also require them to resign their positions or face public humiliation. Church leaders are often forced—or force themselves—to promote or support things they no longer actually believe in.

There have been exceptions. When bestselling author Jen Hatmaker announced her support for same-sex marriage and encouraged Christians to be more inclusive of LGBTQ individuals and communities, the backlash was swift. She was inundated with all sorts of resistance and bullying, and Life-Way Christian bookstores pulled her books from its shelves. Instead of being lauded for her honesty, she was ruthlessly attacked. What Hatmaker did was what countless Christians had already done and are doing: changed her mind. But most of us don't have to consider broadcasting such decisions to tens of thousands of people. Our changing minds aren't tied to the risk of losing our livelihoods.

Jesus' entire message was a radical proclamation of change and transformation. We must remember that "he who began a good work in you will bring it to completion at the day of Jesus Christ" (Philippians 1:6). We must thank God that we are "being transformed into the same image from one degree of glory to another. For this comes from the Lord who is the Spirit" (2 Corinthians 3:18).

Jesus was rejected by the religious leaders of his day for changing the world around him, and his disciples were relentlessly persecuted and martyred for exchanging societal norms for the upside-down lifestyle of following Jesus. They believed in a revolutionary spiritual concept that revolved around the very idea of change: that God incarnate came down to earth and suffered as a human, and that this person was named Jesus. The new has come, the old has gone. A life-altering change has occurred and is occurring.

Being open to change—healthy, life-giving, and positive change—is essential to surviving the marathon of following Jesus. As the apostle Paul writes, "Be transformed by the renewal of your mind, that by testing you may discern what is the will of God, what is good and acceptable and perfect" (Romans 12:2).

10

Is There Hope beyond the Reckoning?

But God shows his love for us in that while we were still sinners, Christ died for us.
—ROMANS 5:8

When visiting missionaries weren't using me as an object lesson for spiritual failure, I found attending a nondenominational Pentecostal church to be fun and sometimes just plain crazy. People were emotional, worship was flamboyant and unpredictable, and services would sometimes go hours into the night.

Imagine being a third grader and witnessing the everyday norms of a Holy Spirit–filled church: people speaking in tongues, waving their hands up in the air, doing interpretive dances, twirling flags during worship, shaking tambourines, being slain in the Spirit, convulsing on the ground, prophesying, crying, wailing, and yelling. There was movement, energy, and uncontrollable action.

Then there were my parents.

While the fire-breathing wind of the Holy Spirit engulfed the sanctuary in charismatic chaos, my mom and dad stood still. Stoic and unmoved, with no visible emotion. People would be shaking right next to us, literally rolling around on the floor and yelling in tongues. But no matter; my parents would be standing like the Queen's Guard—unaffected by their surroundings, staring straight ahead, arms at their sides.

As a self-conscious and sensitive child, I was painfully aware that my parents were out of place. As everyone became swept away by the fervor of the Holy Spirit, I felt embarrassingly awkward—standing alongside my parents, the three of us like silent sentinels, while everyone else did everything but stand still.

Eventually the church service would end, the congregation would be dismissed, and people would go home and resume their daily lives. And it was outside of church, at some point, that I noticed that my parents were actually not normal—either by the charismatic standards of our church or by the ladder-climbing values of our neighbors. It was when my parents left church on Sunday that I truly witnessed their counter-cultural lifestyle and commitment to Christ.

They volunteered to give rides to people who didn't have cars. They delivered meals to the hungry. They housed those needing shelter and generously but quietly donated money to those struggling financially.

They also didn't do a lot of things—like gossip, cheat, swear, or lie. But they didn't just *not* do certain things; they actively *did* things that mattered in the lives of people. In tangible acts of Christlike love, my parents were living out their faith.

There's a difference between participating in Christian traditions and actually living like Christ. Throughout my church experiences I've known Christians who have cheated on their spouses, who were addicted to drugs and pornography, and who did horrible things. I've also known Christians who gave away their wealth and selflessly served the world around them. I've seen churchgoers do wicked acts and good deeds—and sometimes it was the same people who did both.

This is church, where there can be a lot of religious posturing and superficiality but also an abundance of authenticity and love. Despite everything, God resides within all this turmoil. God lives here with us, in the rubble of a failing Christendom.

For there is no such thing as a perfect church community. Even the early church of the New Testament, whose example many modern Christians use as the ideal blueprint for spiritual community, had major issues. Entire books of the Bible were written with the primary purpose of correcting early church Christians and pointing out what they were doing wrong. To the churches in Galatia, Paul admonishes, "I am astonished that you are so quickly deserting him who called you in the grace of Christ and are turning to a different gospel" (Galatians 1:6), and to the churches in Corinth he urges, "I appeal to you, brothers, by the name of our Lord Jesus Christ, that all of you agree, and that there be no divisions among you, but that you be united in the same mind and the same judgment. For it has been reported to me by Chloe's people that there is quarreling among you" (1 Corinthians 1:10-11). According to Paul, even the earliest Christian communities struggled to get it right.

This book has been about coming to terms with disillusionment. In it I have tried to reckon with the sins of the church honestly. But my hope is that this book will help to reconstruct your faith. By identifying the negative attributes of contemporary Christian culture, especially white evangelicalism, we can live toward the holy attributes of Christ. Although Christians are associated with many bad things, we need not disassociate ourselves from Christianity itself. We cannot dismiss all of Christianity because of the actions of some. Like my parents, who didn't always fit in their church community but who nonetheless chose to live out their faith every day of the week, we can choose to follow Jesus in tangible, embodied ways. God holds us accountable for our actions; so too should we care enough about Christianity to hold it to the highest of standards—one that brings about life, justice, love, and righteousness.

And what does a righteous life look like? Say it all together now: It looks like the life of Christ.

So how can we find hope for surviving a Christianity that looks nothing like Christ? In Christ himself, who models for us sacrificial and unconditional love. Let's look at a few ways to hold on to hope for the contemporary church. All of these require stepping out in faith, and trust, and compassion to follow Jesus. "To be a Christian is to live dangerously, honestly, freely," writes Cornel West. To be a Christian, he says, is "to step in the name of love as if you may land on nothing, yet to keep on stepping because the something that sustains you no empire can give you and no empire can take away."[1]

LEARN FROM CHRIST-FOLLOWERS AT THE MARGINS

Being with the marginalized was the very heart of Jesus' ministry. The majority culture—that of the Romans—and the religious power-holders—the Pharisees—attempted to stop

Jesus as he advocated for others, but in the end, sacrificial love overcomes the power of religious empires. "It is marginalized voices that may be the very ones that communicate *best* what kingdom values are," says scholar and pastor Dennis Edwards. "Jesus himself was on the margins. We need to ask ourselves: what does it mean to be a disciple of Jesus knowing he himself, the one we follow and imitate, was on the margins?"[2] In fact, if we aren't listening to the marginalized and defending the oppressed, we are failing as followers of Jesus.

For white Christians, this means taking intentional steps. Beverly Tatum, author of *Why Are All the Black Kids Sitting Together in the Cafeteria?*, suggests that white people need to "start to learn what whiteness means," and can do so by entering spaces—classrooms, churches, workplaces—that are racially mixed environments. By doing so, she says, "you start to see what racial-group membership means for other people."[3]

As Christians, we must actively create windows from our lives into the lives of those who have experienced injustice so we can witness the reality of others. While books, documentaries, articles, and other forms of media certainly are helpful, nothing is more powerful than listening to—and understanding—someone else's personal story. This doesn't mean others have an obligation to explain to you their experiences or be ambassadors of their culture. Doing this puts the responsibility of understanding on others rather than ourselves. But when individuals talk about being called derogatory terms, followed while shopping, and pulled over again and again by police officers, take their words and stories to heart. Windows that help us see beyond ourselves help us comprehend the realities of racial profiling, systemic racism, and various social injustices.

The great paradox of Christianity is that the oppressed become the most prophetic in their ministry and influence—calling the privileged church to repentance and accountability. Christianity's legacy includes revolutionaries and colonialists, slaves and slave owners, pacifists and soldiers, and is as complex and convoluted as the people who represent it. Throughout the church's sullied history are battered communities who boldly proclaimed the unadulterated love of Christ. They still do today. So while some crave—and attain—carnal power, they simultaneously lose their spiritual potency. Denominations have risen and fallen, and spiritual movements have ebbed and flowed, providing both good and bad consequences. The lesson we need to learn is that the love of Christ is always the better way. It's better than political power and societal control. It's better than legislative legalism and economic fortune. This divine love is best manifested by emulating Jesus, by giving to other people who are divinely made in God's image—by loving humanity, especially those most different from ourselves.

"If you call yourself part of the church community at large and locally, be a part of it for the Jesus of the gospel, who makes a way for us to do this difficult work," writes Kaitlin Curtice, who is an enrolled member of the Potawatomi Citizen Band Nation and knows well the legacy of colonizing Christianity. "Be a part of the decolonizing church, the oppression-breaking church, the totally humble church."[4]

LEAN INTO YOUR CITIZENSHIP IN THE KINGDOM OF GOD
When you recognize that you are a citizen of the kingdom of God, your priorities shift. Trying to climb up the corporate ladder faster or to sock away more money for retirement

suddenly becomes less important and less urgent than helping others. Money and fame become secondary desires, and the Holy Spirit redirects us to be more relational: to talk to the coworker we know is struggling, to mentor a student, to work for the change of unjust laws. The goal of life no longer revolves around bettering ourselves but becomes focused on uplifting others.

Jesus announced, repeatedly, that he came to usher in the kingdom of God. "The Kingdom of God is what we all of us hunger for above all other things even when we don't know its name or realize that it's what we're starving to death for," writes Frederick Buechner. "The Kingdom of God is where we belong. It is home, and whether we realize it or not, I think we are all of us homesick for it."[5]

Instead of looking at the world as consumers searching for wealth, or as Democrats or Republicans, or as U.S. citizens or Canadians, people who seek after the kingdom start seeing things first as Christ-followers. This paradigm shift reworks everything you once valued and makes delivering the good news—the love of Christ—the new framework from which you're inspired. A citizen in the kingdom of God is who you were meant to be. As a follower of Christ, this is who you are. You're part of the divine kingdom that is built through the supernatural power of an endlessly loving God.

Gregory Boyd captures the contrasts of the kingdom of God versus the kingdom of the world:

> Participants in the kingdom of the world trust the power of the sword to control behavior; participants of the kingdom of God trust the power of self-sacrificial love to transform hearts. The kingdom of the world is concerned with preserving law and order by force; the kingdom of

God is concerned with establishing the rule of God through love. The kingdom of the world is centrally concerned with what people do; the kingdom of God is centrally concerned with how people are and what they can become. The kingdom of the world is characterized by judgment; the kingdom of God is characterized by outrageous, even scandalous, grace.[6]

As citizens of the kingdom of God, we have been given the noblest calling of all: to live a life inspired out of love. We must understand that we can only love God and others because of God's infinite love for us, living within us through the Holy Spirit.

In the kingdom of God, there's neither Jew nor Gentile; no restrictions as to who can receive it or bestow it on others. Any allegiances to political entities add restrictions, inhibiting our ability to see people beyond political labels. Our moral compass and standards of holiness should be informed by our loyalty to Jesus rather than our allegiance to politicians or political parties.

Christians can develop a bad habit of interpreting God through their political platform. For example, adultery is wrong, but when presidents of the United States commit it, Christians tend to react differently depending on which political party they support and who the president is at the time. When it comes to expressing love to others, we can take sides, choosing to withhold it or give it depending on how it may serve our political purposes. This is especially relevant when dealing with the culture wars, in which issues such as immigration, racism, foreign policy, healthcare, gun control, and abortion each stir up strong sectarian emotions. As Christians, we must find a way to let Jesus dictate our politics.

Recovering an authentic vision of Christ often means blinding ourselves to the secondary visions of our favorite political organizations. It also means prioritizing God over the love we have for our country. As followers of Jesus, we have committed ourselves to serving the kingdom of God more than any other empire.

RESIST WITH LOVE

Jesus got angry, and called out injustice, and actively worked to fix a broken world. But he never did so by sinning against others. His power was supreme because it wasn't fueled by violence or political control but by a sacrificial love that never ceased.

There's much to be angry about with regard to culturally and politically dominant Christianity. It's tempting to try to right wrongs by implementing the same methods that many Christians have used in the past: grasping at power and wielding influence. Political maneuvering may gain us power, name-calling may prick others' pride, bullying could weaken their resolve, and excluding could isolate their influence. But nothing will bring about the kingdom of God other than Christlike love. The apostle Paul writes, "For the sake of Christ, then, I am content with weaknesses, insults, hardships, persecutions, and calamities. For when I am weak, then I am strong" (2 Corinthians 12:10). When Jesus came to earth, he showed us a new and better way to obtain strength.

When we interact with others who disagree with us or when we grow angry or are overwhelmed by disappointment at the state of the church, reminding ourselves that love is the law of the kingdom of God can help us reframe the way we think and act. When we engage using cultural norms—by breaking people down through insults or controlling them through coercive power—we're forsaking Christ. To respond like Christ—with love and love and more love—takes immense practice and discipline.

The way of Jesus is love and healing. Jesus rebuked the disciple who used a sword to cut off the soldier's ear. Jesus healed the man's ear, loving his enemy (Luke 22:50-51). When facing mobs, such as those who were ready to stone and kill a woman caught in adultery, Jesus didn't engage by picking up stones. Instead, he quietly drew in the sand (John 8:1-11). Jesus said, "Blessed are the peacemakers" (Matthew 5:9).

"Love, embraced as a guiding orientation of other-centeredness, will always lead us to do the right thing," writes Bruxy Cavey. "To make his point about love replacing law, Jesus sets out to deconstruct the rule-based system of the religion of his day. Before he can build for people a new understanding of a love-led life, he first has to tear down the old law-based edifice. So Jesus lives in such a way as to offend those who put their faith in religious rules rather than in the way of love."[7]

The idea that we should let love guide our lives can be easy to understand but complicated to apply. And love does not preclude criticism and resistance. When Jesus critiqued the religious leaders of his day, their initial reaction was to deny his allegations and fight back. Today's churches could learn a lot from Jesus, an activist who called for reform. We can be loving critics of church institutions and churches that are failing to live up to their identity in Christ. With love as our guide, we can call the church and other Christ-followers to remember the Savior who stands at the center of our faith.

FIND A SUPPORTIVE COMMUNITY

If you belong to a Christian community that is pursuing Christendom rather than Christ, you may need to look for a community that emulates Jesus. If you are exhausted and frustrated to the point of cynicism, you may need to pray and reflect on whether you are in the right place. Seek counsel from wise Christ-followers within and outside of your community.

As I reflect on the highs and lows of my spiritual journey, there's a close correlation between the spiritual health of the community in which I was involved and the state of my discipleship to Christ. During the lows, those in my surrounding faith community—and I as well—were not being like Jesus. My relationships were selfish, tinged with insecurity and superficiality. But during the highs of my faith journey—and sometimes those highs happened even amid the toughest of times—a Christlike community empowered me. Often it wasn't my ability to trust in God's love that carried me through obstacles; instead, other people carried me through. It was their trust in God's love that enabled them to carry me.

If you haven't found such a community, try joining an online one. A virtual community is no replacement for a local body of believers, and there are drawbacks to digital forms of community, but social media and other ways of connecting online do offer Christians the opportunity to create meaningful friendships. As a blogger, I've seen firsthand how online communities can foster a spirituality that is honest and vibrant. You can learn from diverse voices of faith online. Since the average person typically spends much of the day online, it makes sense that we would take the opportunity to deepen our faith there too.

REMEMBER HOW MUCH GOD LOVES YOU

God's very essence can be seen through Christ and known through the Holy Spirit. Whatever your opinions or beliefs about Christianity, know this: God is unchanging, God is good, and God loves you more than you can possibly imagine. There are many religions that claim to own God, churches that try to sell God, politicians who promote their love for God, and an endless number of people searching for God. But if you want to love and be loved by God, look to Jesus. Read the gospel accounts of a divine being who came to earth and truly loved humanity to the point of willingly dying for them—for *you*.

My parents showed me that God's love still existed. My best friends showed me God's grace. A stranger showed me that divine sacrifice was real. An enemy showed me the beauty of divine forgiveness. My college roommate showed me that authentic fellowship was achievable. My wife showed me that faith wasn't just a theory. A stranger showed me God's kindness.

An invitation to coffee. A text. A gift. A prepared meal. A compliment. An apology. A Christian community gives of itself for the sake of others. God's love is made manifest through our sisters and brothers in Christ.

If you are a follower of Christ, you have the power of the Holy Spirit. You are a representative of something holy, divine, and godly, and you are capable of producing supernatural goodness. Just as a culturally dominant Christianity can ruin God's reputation by being hypocritical and oppressive, Christ-followers can glorify God and make God truly known.

Right here and right now, Jesus is with you, waiting to speak to you, be with you, and communicate with you. So as you figure out what parts of dominant cultural Christianity you must reject, please don't make the mistake of rejecting Christ. Christ has already accepted you as you are, and he is waiting for you to accept him back.

Go into the world knowing that God is love and that God loves you. Be loved.

Notes

1. DISILLUSIONED

1 Sarah Bessey, "On Being a Christian and Being a Feminist . . . and Belonging Nowhere," *Sarah Bessey* (blog), January 24, 2017, www.sarahbessey.com/christian-feminist/.

2 For more on contemporary evangelicalism, see Mark Labberton, ed., *Still Evangelical? Insiders Reconsider Political, Social, and Theological Meaning* (Downers Grove, IL: InterVarsity Press, 2018).

3 Christopher Hitchens, *God Is Not Great: How Religion Poisons Everything* (London: Atlantic Books, 2017), 13. First published 2007.

4 Peter Hitchens, *The Rage against God* (London: Continuum, 2012), 90. First published 2010.

5 Adolf Hitler, *Mein Kampf* (Boston: Houghton Mifflin, 1971), 65. First published 1925.

6 Frederick Douglass, appendix to *Narrative of the Life of Frederick Douglass, An American Slave, Written by Himself* (Boston: Anti-Slavery Office, 1845), 117.

7 Quoted in Noel Rae, *The Great Stain: Witnessing American Slavery* (New York: Overlook Press, 2018), 202.

8 Adam Lusher, "Waco: How a 51-Day Standoff Between a Christian Cult and the FBI Left More Than 80 Dead and Divided America," *The Independent*, January 26, 2018, www.independent.co.uk/news/world/americas/waco-tv-series-siege-truth-what-really-happened-david-koresh-branch-davidians-cult-fbi-paramount-a8179936.html.

9 Jason Nark, "Guns and Religion Mix as Pa. Church Blesses Couples Toting AR-15s," Philly.com, March 1, 2018, www.philly.com/philly/news/pennsylvania/pennsylvania-church-blessing-ar-15-guns-rifles-poconos-20180228.html.

10 Bruxy Cavey, *The End of Religion: Encountering the Subversive Spirituality of Jesus* (Colorado Springs: NavPress, 2007), 18.

11 W. Island, "Joel Osteen's Reaction to Tropical Storm Harvey Reveals the Pitfalls of Prosperity Gospel," *Huffington Post*, August 31, 2017, https://www.huffingtonpost.com/entry/prosperity-gospel-scam_us_59a761e0e4b02498834a8eac.

12 Erwin Raphael McManus, *Unleashed: Release the Untamed Faith Within* (Nashville: Thomas Nelson, 2011), 127. First published 2006.

13 Kaitlin Curtice, "When the Church Uses God's Name to Oppress," *Sojourners*, March 5, 2018, www.sojo.net/articles/when-church-uses-god-s-name-oppress.

2. SINS OF THE CHURCH

1 Mark M. Gray and Paul M. Perl, *The Sacrament of Reconciliation* (Washington, DC: Center for Applied Research in the Apostolate, April/May 2008).

2 "Five Key Findings on Religion in the U.S.," Gallup, December 23, 2016, http://news.gallup.com/poll/200186/five-key-findings-religion.aspx?g_source=Religion&g_medium=newsfeed&g_campaign=tiles; "Most Americans Still Believe in God," Gallup, June 29, 2016, http://news.gallup.com/poll/193271/americans-believe-god.aspx.

3 "What Americans Think about Women in Power," Barna Group, accessed January 20, 2018, https://www.barna.com/research/americans-think-women-power/.

4 "Distribution of Medical School Graduates by Gender," Henry J. Kaiser Family Foundation, March 2, 2017, https://kaiserf.am/2Jeb1IT; Kathleen Elkins, "20 Jobs That Are Dominated by Women," *Business Insider*, February 17, 2015, www.businessinsider.com/pink-collar-jobs-dominated-by-women-2015-2.

5 These figures can be found at "Statistics," National Coalition Against Domestic Violence (website), accessed May 10, 2018, https://ncadv.org/statistics; "Scope of the Problem: Statistics," RAINN (website), accessed May 10, 2018, https://www.rainn.org/statistics/scope-problem; Jugal K. Patel, Troy Griggs, and Claire Cain Miller, "We Asked 615 Men about How They Conduct Themselves at Work," *New York Times*, December 28, 2017, https://www.nytimes.com/interactive/2017/12/28/upshot/sexual-harassment-survey-600-men.html; Barbara G. Ellis, "The Workplace War: Hatpins Might Be in Style Again for

Women," CounterPunch, January 18, 2018, https://www
.counterpunch.org/2018/01/18/the-workplace-war-
hatpins-might-be-in-style-again-for-women/.

6 Morgan Lee, "My Larry Nassar Testimony Went Viral.
But There's More to the Gospel Than Forgiveness,"
Christianity Today, January 31, 2018, www.christianity-
today.com/ct/2018/january-web-only/rachael-
denhollander-larry-nassar-forgiveness-gospel.html.

7 "Read Rachael Denhollander's Full Victim Impact
Statement about Larry Nassar," CNN, January 30, 2018,
www.cnn.com/2018/01/24/us/rachael-denhollander-
full-statement/.

8 Gregory A. Smith and Jessica Martínez, "How the Faithful Voted: A Preliminary 2016 Analysis," Pew Research
Center, November 9, 2016, www.pewresearch.org/fact-
tank/2016/11/09/how-the-faithful-voted-a-preliminary-
2016-analysis/; "Transcript: Donald Trump's Taped
Comments about Women," *New York Times*, October 8,
2016, https://www.nytimes.com/2016/10/08/us/donald-
trump-tape-transcript.html.

9 Kyle Swenson, "A Pastor Admitted a Past 'Sexual Incident' with a Teen, Saying He Was 'Deeply Sorry.' His
Congregation Gave Him a Standing Ovation," *Washington Post*, January 10, 2018, www.washingtonpost.com/
news/morning-mix/wp/2018/01/10/a-pastor-admitted-a-
past-sexual-incident-with-a-teen-his-congregation-gave-
him-a-standing-ovation/?utm_term=.4c8b90577f20.
Savage has since stepped down.

10 Martha Rainbolt and Janet Fleetwood, eds., *On the Contrary: Essays by Men and Women* (Albany: State University of New York Press, 1983), 13.

11 Carol L. Higham, "Christian Missions to American Indians," *Oxford Research Encyclopedia of American History*, June 8, 2017, http://americanhistory.oxfordre .com/view/10.1093/acrefore/9780199329175.001.0001/ acrefore-9780199329175-e-323.

12 Bonnie D. Newsom and Jamie Bissonette-Lewey, "Wabanaki Resistance and Healing: An Exploration of the Contemporary Ro," *Landscapes of Violence* 2, no. 1 (2012), http://dx.doi.org/10.7275/R5KW5CXB.

13 Higham, "Christian Missions."

14 Rebecca Onion, "America's Other Original Sin," *Slate*, January 18, 2016, http://www.slate.com/articles/news_ and_politics/cover_story/2016/01/native_american_ slavery_historians_uncover_a_chilling_chapter_in_ u_s_history.html; "Historical Context: Facts about the Slave Trade and Slavery," Gilder Lehrman Institute of American History, accessed May 10, 2018, https://www .gilderlehrman.org/content/historical-context-facts-about- slave-trade-and-slavery. Some 12.5 million Africans were forced into the Middle Passage, but roughly 12 percent did not survive the inhumane conditions of the voyage.

15 Randy S. Woodley, "Shalom and the Community of Cre- ation," *Spirituality and Practice*, accessed April 5, 2018, www.spiritualityandpractice.com/book-reviews/excerpts/ view/23646/shalom-and-the-community-of-creation.

16 "Chinese Exclusion Act (1882)," Immigration to the United States, 1789–1930, Harvard University Library Open Collections Program, accessed January 23, 2018, http://ocp.hul.harvard.edu/immigration/exclusion.html.

17 "Japanese Relocation during World War II," National Archives and Records Administration, accessed January 23, 2018, https://www.archives.gov/education/lessons/japanese-relocation.

18 "History of Lynchings," NAACP, accessed January 22, 2018, www.naacp.org/history-of-lynchings/; "African Americans, Women, and the GI Bill," Khan Academy, accessed January 25, 2018, https://www.khanacademy.org/humanities/ap-us-history/period-8/apush-postwar-era/a/african-americans-women-and-the-gi-bill; Matthew Desmond, *Evicted: Poverty and Profit in the American City* (New York: Broadway Books, 2017).

19 Michelle Alexander, *The New Jim Crow: Mass Incarceration in the Age of Colorblindness*, rev. ed. (New York: New Press, 2012), 183–84.

20 Michael Harriot, "Yes, You Can Measure White Privilege," *The Root*, April 14, 2017, https://www.theroot.com/yes-you-can-measure-white-privilege-1794303451.

21 Jeffrey Cawood, "Black Lives Matter Leader: 'Stop Saying White Privilege and Start Saying White Supremacy,'" Daily Wire, September 3, 2017, https://www.dailywire.com/news/20584/black-lives-matter-leader-stop-saying-white-jeffrey-cawood.

22 Michael S. Kimmel and Abby L. Ferber, *Privilege: A Reader*, 4th ed. (Boulder, CO: Westview Press, 2017), xiv.

23 For more on this, see "Jesus Is Black. Get Over It," *Premier Christianity*, January 30, 2017, https://www .premierchristianity.com/Blog/Jesus-is-black.-Get-over-it; Mike Fillon, "The Real Face of Jesus: Advances in Forensic Science Reveal the Most Famous Face in History," *Popular Mechanics*, December 2002, posted January 22, 2015, http://www.popularmechanics.com/science/health/ a234/1282186/; Christena Cleveland, "Why Jesus' Skin Color Matters," *Christianity Today*, accessed January 23, 2018, http://www.christianitytoday.com/ct/2016/april/ why-jesus-skin-color-matters.html.

24 Mae Elise Cannon, Soong-Chan Rah, Troy Jackson, and Lisa Sharon Harper, *Forgive Us: Confessions of a Compromised Faith* (Grand Rapids, MI: Zondervan, 2014), 72.

25 Amber Cantorna, "Family Matters," *Out Front*, May 18, 2017, https://www.outfrontmagazine.com/trending/ culture/family-matters-amber-cantorna/.

26 Kapya Kaoma, "How Anti-Gay Christians Evangelize Hate Abroad," *Los Angeles Times*, March 23, 2014, http://www.latimes.com/opinion/op-ed/la-oe-kaoma- uganda-gays-american-ministers-20140323-story.html; David Smith, "Why Africa is the Most Homophobic Continent," *The Observer*, February 22, 2014, https://www.theguardian.com/world/2014/feb/23/ africa-homophobia-uganda-anti-gay-law.

27 Matthew Vines, *God and the Gay Christian: The Biblical Case in Support of Same-Sex Relationships* (New York: Convergent Books, 2015), 11.

28 Jeremy J. Gibbs, "Religious Conflict, Sexual Identity, and Suicidal Behaviors among LGBT Young Adults," *Archives of Suicide Research* 19, no. 4 (2015): 472–88.

29 David P. Gushee, *Changing Our Mind* (Canton, MI: Read the Spirit Books, 2017), 11–12. First published 2014.

30 Justin Lee, *Torn: Rescuing the Gospel from the Gays-vs.-Christians Debate* (New York: Jericho Books, 2013), 16.

31 Jeff Diamant and Becka A. Alper, "Though Still Conservative, Young Evangelicals Are More Liberal Than Their Elders on Some Issues," Pew Research Center, May 4, 2017, http://www.pewresearch.org/fact-tank/2017/05/04/though-still-conservative-young-evangelicals-are-more-liberal-than-their-elders-on-some-issues/.

32 Sarah Coakley, *God, Sexuality, and the Self: An Essay on the Trinity* (New York: Cambridge University Press, 2013), 31.

33 For a glimpse at this list, see "A List of Some of the More Than #2000Verses in Scripture on Poverty and Justice," *Sojourners*, November 29, 2017, https://sojo.net/list-some-more-2000verses-scripture-poverty-and-justice.

34 "Statistics on U.S. Generosity," Philanthropy Roundtable, accessed January 22, 2018, http://www.philanthropy-roundtable.org/almanac/statistics/; Alexia Fernández Campbell, "Why Are Americans Less Charitable Than They Used to Be?" *The Atlantic*, December 27, 2016, https://www.theatlantic.com/business/archive/2016/12/americans-donate-less-to-charity/511397/.

35 Boz Tchividjian, "Startling Statistics: Child Sexual Abuse and What the Church Can Begin Doing about It," Religion News Service, January 9, 2014, https://religionnews .com/2014/01/09/startling-statistics/; "Child Sexual Abuse Statistics," National Center for Victims of Crime, accessed January 23, 2018, http:// victimsofcrime.org/media/reporting-on-child-sexual-abuse/child-sexual-abuse-statistics.

36 Madison Park, "Timeline: A Look at the Catholic Church's Sex Abuse Scandals," CNN, June 29, 2017, https://www.cnn.com/2017/06/29/world/timeline-catholic-church-sexual-abuse-scandals/index.html.

37 Christopher Knaus, "Victims Say Catholic Church Data on Child Abuse Underestimates Scale of Offending," *The Guardian*, February 5, 2017, https://www.theguardian. com/australia-news/2017/feb/06/victims-say-catholic-church-data-on-child-abuse-underestimates-scale-of-offending.

38 "Child Refugee and Migrant Crisis," UNICEF USA, accessed January 24, 2018, https://www.unicefusa.org/ mission/emergencies/child-refugees.

39 Gregory A. Smith, "Most White Evangelicals Approve of Trump Travel Prohibition and Express Concerns about Extremism," Pew Research Center, February 27, 2017, http://www.pewresearch.org/fact-tank/2017/02/27/most-white-evangelicals-approve-of-trump-travel-prohibition-and-express-concerns-about-extremism/.

40 Kelly Rosati, "How to Address America's Foster Care Crisis? It Takes a Village," CT Women, May 27, 2016, https://www.christianitytoday.com/women/2016/may/ why-churches-are-key-to-addressing-americas-foster-care-cri.html.

41 "Foster Care," Children's Rights, accessed January 24,
    2018, http://www.childrensrights.org/newsroom/fact-
    sheets/foster-care/.

42 David Brock, *The Republican Noise Machine: Right-
    Wing Media and How It Corrupts Democracy* (New
    York: Three Rivers Press, 2005), 192.

43 "Nearly 1 in 5 People Have a Disability in the U.S., Cen-
    sus Bureau Reports," U.S. Census Bureau, May 19, 2016,
    https://www.census.gov/newsroom/releases/archives/
    miscellaneous/cb12-134.html; Victoria Bekiempis,
    "Nearly 1 in 5 Americans Suffers from Mental Illness
    Each Year," *Newsweek*, February 28, 2014, http://www
    .newsweek.com/nearly-1-5-americans-suffer-mental-
    illness-each-year-230608; "Any Anxiety Disorder,"
    National Institute of Mental Health, accessed January
    23, 2018, https://www.nimh.nih.gov/health/statistics/
    any-anxiety-disorder.shtml.

44 David Briggs, "Churches Seen as Failing to Welcome
    People with Disabilities," *Christian Century*, August 5,
    2014, https://www.christiancentury.org/article/2014-07/
    churches-seen-failing-welcome-people-disabilities.

45 George F. White, "People with Disabilities in Christian
    Community," *Journal of the Christian Institute on
    Disability* 3, no. 1 (Spring-Summer 2014).

46 Quoted in Roy E. Barsness, "Beyond the Mirror:
    On Desiring God's Mental Health Tweet," *Sojourn-
    ers*, February 14, 2018, https://sojo.net/articles/
    beyond-mirror-desiring-gods-mental-health-tweet.

47 White, "People with Disabilities."

48 Soong-Chan Rah, *Prophetic Lament: A Call for Justice in Troubled Times* (Downers Grove, IL: InterVarsity Press, 2015), 22.

49 Quoted in Michelle Norris, "Writer Anne Rice: 'Today I Quit Being a Christian,'" National Public Radio, August 2, 2010, https://www.npr.org/templates/story/story.php?storyId=128930526.

3. WHEN CHRISTIANITY HURTS

1 Philip Yancey, *Disappointment with God: Three Questions No One Asks Aloud* (Grand Rapids, MI: Zondervan, 2015), 111. First published 1988.

2 Quoted in Shane Claiborne, *The Irresistible Revolution: Living as an Ordinary Radical*, rev. ed. (Grand Rapids, MI: Zondervan, 2016), 58.

3 Samantha Neal, "Views of Racism as a Major Problem Increase Sharply, Especially among Democrats," Pew Research Center, August 29, 2017, http://www.pew research.org/fact-tank/2017/08/29/views-of-racism-as-a-major-problem-increase-sharply-especially-among-democrats/.

4 Shaun King, "Everything That Claims to Be Christian," Medium, September 6, 2015, https://medium.com/theology-of-ferguson/everything-that-claims-to-be-christianity-8dc34001625b.

5 Soong-Chan Rah, *Prophetic Lament: A Call for Justice in Troubled Times* (Downers Grove, IL: InterVarsity Press, 2015), 51.

6 Francis I, *Evangelii gaudium*, apostolic exhortation, November 24, 2013, https://w2.vatican.va/content/

francesco/en/apost_exhortations/documents/papa-
francesco_esortazione-ap_20131124_evangelii-gaudium
.html.

7 Benjamin L. Corey, *Unafraid: Moving beyond Fear-Based
   Faith* (San Francisco: HarperOne, 2017), 7.

8 Beth Moore, *So Long, Insecurity: You've Been a Bad
   Friend to Us* (Carol Stream, IL: Tyndale, 2010), 329.

9 Helen Ellerbe, *The Dark Side of Christian History*
   (San Rafael, CA: Morningstar and Lark, 2004), 6. First
   published 1995.

10 Cornel West, "The Moral Obligations of Living in a
   Democratic Society," chap. 1 in *The Good Citizen*, ed.
   David B. Batstone and Eduardo Mendieta (New York:
   Routledge, 2001), 12.

11 Stanley Hauerwas, *Hannah's Child: A Theologian's Memoir* (Grand Rapids, MI: Eerdmans, 2010), 115.

4. GREAT EXPECTATIONS

1 "Sharia Law, Slavery and Abolishing Amendments: 6 of
   Roy Moore's Most Memorable Quotes," *USA Today*,
   December 12, 2017, https://www.usatoday.com/story/
   news/politics/onpolitics/2017/12/12/sharia-law-slavery-
   6-roy-moores-most-memorable-quotes/943955001/;
   see also Carol Kuruvilla, "White Evangelicals Voted
   En Masse for Roy Moore in Alabama, To No One's
   Surprise," *Huffington Post*, December 14, 2017, https://
   www.huffingtonpost.com/entry/white-evangelicals-voted-
   en-masse-for-roy-moore-in-alabama-to-no-ones-surprise_
   us_5a314abee4b01bdd7659366c.

2 "The State of the Church 2016," Barna Group, accessed January 21, 2018, https://www.barna.com/research/ state-church-2016/.

3 "This Christmas, 78% of Americans Identify as Christian," Gallup, December 24, 2009, http://news.gallup .com/poll/124793/this-christmas-78-americans-identify- christian.aspx.

4 Tom Phillips, "China on Course to Become 'World's Most Christian Nation' within 15 years," *The Telegraph*, April 19, 2014, http://www.telegraph.co.uk/news/worldnews/ asia/china/10776023/China-on-course-to-become- worlds-most-Christian-nation-within-15-years.html.

5 David McClendon, "Sub-Saharan Africa Will Be Home to Growing Shares of the World's Christians and Muslims," Pew Research Center, April 19, 2017, http://www .pewresearch.org/fact-tank/2017/04/19/sub-saharan- africa-will-be-home-to-growing-shares-of-the-worlds- christians-and-muslims/.

6 Brian Zahnd, *A Farewell to Mars: An Evangelical Pastor's Journey toward the Biblical Gospel of Peace* (Colorado Springs: David C. Cook, 2014), 32.

7 "Statistics on U.S. Generosity," *Almanac of American Philanthropy*, accessed February 11, 2018, http://www. philanthropyroundtable.org/almanac/statistics/; Paul Singer, "Faith Groups Provide the Bulk of Disaster Recovery, in Coordination with FEMA," *USA Today*, September 13, 2017, https://www.usatoday.com/story/ news/politics/2017/09/10/hurricane-irma-faith-groups- provide-bulk-disaster-recovery-coordination-fema/ 651007001/.

5. WHY THE IMAGE OF GOD MATTERS

1 Brennan Manning, *The Ragamuffin Gospel* (Colorado Springs: Multnomah Books, 2015), 17–18. First published 1990.

2 Carlos A. Rodríguez, *Drop the Stones: When Love Reaches the Unlovable* (New Kensington, PA: Whitaker House, 2017), 122.

3 Christena Cleveland, *Disunity in Christ: Uncovering the Hidden Forces That Keep Us Apart* (Downers Grove, IL: InterVarsity Press, 2013), 13.

4 Makoto Fujimura, *Culture Care: Reconnecting with Beauty for Our Common Life* (Downers Grove, IL: InterVarsity Press, 2017), 59.

5 "Race, Religion, and Political Affiliation of Americans' Core Social Networks," PRRI, August 3, 2016, https://www.prri.org/research/poll-race-religion-politics-americans-social-networks/.

6 Cleveland, *Disunity in Christ*, 149.

7 Austin Channing Brown, *I'm Still Here: Black Dignity in a World Made for Whiteness* (New York: Convergent, 2018), 65.

8 Quoted in Jann Aldredge-Clanton, "'Embracing the Other,' presentation by Grace Ji-Sun Kim at Christian Feminism Today Gathering," *Grace Ji-Sun Kim* (blog), August 17, 2016, https://gracejisunkim.wordpress.com/2016/08/17/embracing-the-other-presentation-by-grace-ji-sun-kim-at-christian-feminism-today-gathering/.

9 Emily Style, "Curriculum as Window and Mirror," National SEED Project, accessed April 11, 2018,

https://nationalseedproject.org/curriculum-as-window-and-mirror.

6. HOW TO AVOID FOLLOWING JESUS

1 Sarah Perez, "U.S. Consumers Now Spend 5 Hours per Day on Mobile Devices," TechCrunch, March 3, 2017, https://techcrunch.com/2017/03/03/u-s-consumers-now-spend-5-hours-per-day-on-mobile-devices/; "New Research Sheds Light on Daily Ad Exposures," SJ Insights, September 29, 2014, https://sjinsights.net/2014/09/29/new-research-sheds-light-on-daily-ad-exposures/.

2 Lisa Miller, "Is Gun Ownership Christian?" *Washington Post*, January 22, 2013, https://www.washingtonpost.com/local/is-gun-ownership-christian/2013/01/25/c7afe7fe-6724-11e2-93e1-475791032daf_story.html?utm_term=.42429061b131.

3 Jonathan Merritt, "Jerry Falwell Jr.'s Troubling Remarks on Guns," *The Atlantic*, December 6, 2015, https://www.theatlantic.com/politics/archive/2015/12/jerry-falwell-jrs-troubling-remarks-on-guns/419019/.

4 "Guns in the US: The Statistics behind the Violence," BBC News, January 5, 2016, http://www.bbc.com/news/world-us-canada-34996604. This figure excludes suicides.

5 International Physicians for the Prevention of Nuclear War, "Facts about Small Arms and Light Weapons," March 14, 2011, http://ippnw.org/pdf/SmallArmsFacts.pdf.

6 Mike Stone and Matt Spetalnick, "Exclusive: Trump Administration Prepares to Ease Export Rules for U.S." Reuters, September 19, 2017,

https://www.reuters.com/article/us-usa-trump-weapons-exclusive/exclusive-trump-administration-prepares-to-ease-export-rules-for-u-s-guns-idUSKCN1BU2N8.

7 Gary Younge, *Another Day in the Death of America: A Chronicle of Ten Short Lives* (New York: Nation Books, 2018), 7.

8 "Stopping the Trade in Small Arms and Light Weapons," TRAKNAT, accessed January 22, 2018, http://www.traknat.org.uk/tk/?p=357.

9 "Different Faiths, Different Messages," Pew Research Center, March 19, 2003, http://www.people-press.org/2003/03/19/different-faiths-different-messages/.

10 "Religious Groups Issue Statements on War with Iraq," Pew Research Center, March 19, 2003, http://www.pewforum.org/2003/03/19/publicationpage-aspxid616/.

11 "Most Favor Continued U.S. Presence in Afghanistan," National Association of Evangelicals, August 2010, http://www.nae.net/most-favor-continued-u-s-presence-in-afghanistan/.

12 "Less Support for Death Penalty, Especially among Democrats," Pew Research Center, April 16, 2015, http://www.people-press.org/2015/04/16/less-support-for-death-penalty-especially-among-democrats/.

13 Ibid.; "New Position of National Association of Evangelicals Shows Cracks in Death Penalty Support," Death Penalty Information Center, accessed January 26, 2018, https://deathpenaltyinfo.org/node/6279.

14 Shane Claiborne, *Executing Grace: How the Death Penalty Killed Jesus and Why It's Killing Us* (New York: HarperOne, 2016), 4.

15 Michael Lipka and John Gramlich, "5 Facts about Abortion," Pew Research Center, January 26, 2017, http://www.pewresearch.org/fact-tank/2017/01/26/5-facts-about-abortion/; "Abortion Fast Facts," CNN, May 28, 2017, http://www.cnn.com/2013/09/18/health/abortion-fast-facts/.

16 Jo Saxton, "Where Is the Salt? Where Is the Light?" *Jo Saxton* (blog), July 8, 2016, www.josaxton.com/2016/07/08/where-is-the-salt-where-is-the-light/.

17 Rachel Held Evans, *A Year of Biblical Womanhood: How a Liberated Woman Found Herself Sitting on Her Roof, Covering Her Head, and Calling Her Husband "Master"* (Nashville: Thomas Nelson, 2012), 296.

18 As quoted by Shane Claiborne, *The Irresistible Revolution: Living as an Ordinary Radical*, 10th anniv. ed. (Grand Rapids, MI: Zondervan, 2016), 86–87.

7. CITIZENS OF ANOTHER COUNTRY

1 Ted Grimsrud, "Romans 13: An Interpretation," *Peace Theology: Engaging Faith and Pacifism* (blog), last modified June 3, 2008, https://peacetheology.net/pacifism/9-romans-13-an-interpretation/.

2 Gregory A. Boyd, *The Myth of a Christian Nation: How the Quest for Political Power Is Destroying the Church* (Grand Rapids, MI: Zondervan, 2009), 81.

3 Ibid., 80.

9. THE CHRISTIAN VIRTUE OF CHANGE

1 Gregory A. Boyd, "How to Talk about Theology," ReKnew, June 2, 2015, www.reknew.org/2014/06/how-to-talk-about-theology/.

2 Ibid.

3 David Kinnaman and Gabe Lyons, *UnChristian: What a New Generation Really Thinks about Christianity . . . and Why It Matters* (Grand Rapids, MI: Baker Books, 2012), 83. First published 2007.

10. IS THERE HOPE BEYOND THE RECKONING?

1 Cornel West, *Democracy Matters: Winning the Fight against Imperialism* (New York: Penguin Books, 2005), 98.

2 Dennis R. Edwards, "Dennis Edwards on Letting the Marginalized Lead Us," interview by Shane Blackshear, Missio Alliance, December 20, 2017, http://www.missioalliance.org/dennis-edwards-letting-marginalized-lead-us-interview-shane-blackshear/.

3 Quoted in Melinda D. Anderson, "Do Conversations about Race Belong in the Classroom?" *The Atlantic*, September 5, 2017, www.theatlantic.com/education/archive/2017/09/beverly-daniel-tatum-classroom-conversations-race/538758/.

4 Kaitlin Curtice, "When the Church Uses God's Name to Oppress," *Sojourners*, March 5, 2018, http://www.sojo.net/articles/when-church-uses-god-s-name-oppress.

5 Frederick Buechner, *Secrets in the Dark: A Life in Sermons* (New York: HarperOne, 2007), 149.

6 Gregory A. Boyd, *The Myth of a Christian Nation: How the Quest for Political Power Is Destroying the Church* (Grand Rapids, MI: Zondervan, 2009), 31.

7 Bruxy Cavey, *The End of Religion: Encountering the Subversive Spirituality of Jesus* (Colorado Springs: NavPress, 2007), 49.

The Author

Stephen Mattson is a writer and activist whose work has been published in *Relevant*, *Huffington Post*, *Sojourners*, Red Letter Christians, and a variety of other venues. Mattson graduated from Moody Bible Institute, served as a youth pastor, and now works at University of Northwestern–St. Paul. He and his wife and children live near Saint Paul, Minnesota, and attend Woodland Hills Church.